The Art
of the Click

The *Art* of the Click

How to harness the power of direct-response copywriting and make more sales

Glenn Fisher

Hh Harriman House

HARRIMAN HOUSE LTD
18 College Street
Petersfield
Hampshire
GU31 4AD
GREAT BRITAIN
Tel: +44 (0)1730 233870
Email: enquiries@harriman-house.com
Website: www.harriman-house.com

First published in Great Britain in 2018
Copyright © Glenn Fisher

Paperback ISBN: 978-0-85719-694-1
eBook ISBN: 978-0-85719-695-8

British Library Cataloguing in Publication Data
A CIP catalogue record for this book can be obtained from the British Library.

For Ruth Wilde who makes me laugh every day

With thanks to Wendy Fisher who bankrolled my
Dick Whittington moment

Every owner of a physical copy of this edition of

The Art of the Click

can download the eBook for free direct from us at Harriman House, in a format that can be read on any eReader, tablet or smartphone.

Simply head to:

ebooks.harriman-house.com/artoftheclick

to get your free eBook now.

Contents

Part Three – The Interviews

About the author

Glenn Fisher was born in Grimsby in 1981. After a number of years working in the local council, he left to become a copywriter and founded AllGoodCopy.com, a free online resource for direct response copywriters and marketers. For over a decade he worked with The Agora, a huge international financial publisher. In 2018, having helped launch and grow Agora Financial in the UK, he began to write copy on a freelance basis and focus on coaching aspiring copywriters. He now lives happily with his partner Ruth and dog Pablo on the east coast of England.

Preface

What this book is about

The Art of the Click is about using language to persuade people. It's about identifying ideas and expressing them in a way that will engage more people to click on your advert, read your blog or buy your product. It aims to teach you how to do this by exploring the fundamentals of direct-response copywriting.

Direct-response copywriting is something of a forgotten skill, associated largely with the old fashioned concept of direct mail. The association is wrong. The fact is that commerce today increasingly takes place online and sales can be made with the click of a button, yet surprisingly few businesses realise they are working in a direct-response environment. Instead they choose to run-up wild costs focusing on more indirect, abstract and less-measurable concepts such as brand identity, product placement and social influencers.

There is a place for these techniques in marketing your business and such things can have a positive effect on sales. However, this book is not concerned with logos, celebrity or sponsorship. It is concerned with more tangible and, more importantly, *testable* variables any business can influence to make more sales. Specifically it considers the ideas you wish to communicate about your products, it studies the audience receiving them and it shares actionable advice on how to craft messages in a way that increases the likelihood they will be acted upon.

It should be noted that while there is much to be said for using offline marketing channels such as direct mail – especially in such a crowded online marketplace – in the interest of clarity, the book concentrates on all things digital, hence the art of the *click*, not the *coupon*. That said, the ideas and advice shared here can be applied both online and off, not least the study of the long copy sales letter, a seeming relic of the offline era that can teach us a great deal about engaging readers in the internet age.

Finally, this book is about having fun. One of the most effective ways to engage is to entertain. I hope to do that in the pages that follow. Throughout the book, as well as practical advice about writing to sell, you'll also find tasks I recommend you try or field trips you should take to better understand your customers. I encourage you to give everything a go and have fun with it.

Who this book is for

First and foremost, *The Art of the Click* is for anyone who's looking for a secret weapon to help them make more sales. It is not just an instruction manual for copywriters. Whether you're a designer, marketer or business owner, studying and applying the insight and advice that follows will help you be more successful in your role. In that respect, the book is for anyone who wishes to understand more about how people think and how you can use direct-response copywriting to craft your sales message and alter the influence it has on people.

How this book is structured

You'll see the book is broken down into three parts.

The first part explores everything you should consider *before* you attempt to write a single word. We look at the importance of studying successful direct-response copy, researching your audience and, crucially, identifying what makes an idea worth writing about at all.

The second part of the book digs deeper into writing techniques. We look at how to turn features into benefits, how to construct headlines that grab your reader's attention and how to write engaging copy that holds it.

In the third part of the book I share three interviews with expert direct-response copywriters who have had a big influence on my own writing and career. In addition to the tips I share in the book, John Forde, Mark Ford and James Woodburn reveal their own unique insights into how direct-response copywriting can help you.

There is a narrative structure running through the book. However, should you wish to dip in when looking for some inspiration, each chapter can just as easily be read in isolation. Keep this book by your side when you write and it will serve you well.

My hope is that *The Art of the Click* will start a conversation about direct-response copywriting. Though the fundamental principles discussed here are timeless, techniques for executing them are developing all the time. There is always more we can learn about any subject and when you've finished this book I look forward to exploring ideas further together. You can find me talking all things direct-response copywriting on Twitter at @allgoodcopy.

Introduction
Direct-Response Copywriting in the Internet Age

"You really want to get a headache? Try to understand internet advertising."

— *Barry Diller, American businessman*

Click here to see the good stuff

Click here to like this funny image of my dog. Click here to show you agree with my thoughts about this film. Click here to reserve tickets for the gig my band is playing tonight. Click here to sponsor me, to reply to my email, to confirm what time we're meeting. Click here to confirm your order. Click here to read the small print. Click here to see if your size is available. Click here to upgrade to the unlimited drinks package. Click here to watch the next episode, to renew your subscription, to update your bank details. Click here to register your address. Click here to say you've read the T&Cs. And, for heaven's sake, hurry up and click here to claim your urgent free report.

Recognise any of those requests? I'm sure you do. But let me ask you: when was the last time *you* asked someone to do one of those things? Often, without realising it, a day rarely goes by *without* you asking someone to click on something – *either directly or indirectly*. But whether it's a friend on Facebook or a prospect at work, your aim is always the same: to elicit a response and get that click.

It's not easy to get people to click on things. You'll know that if you've ever sat wondering why more people don't like the picture you posted on Instagram of your dog in a flat cap, or why you've only sold one ticket to the 250-capacity personal-finance seminar you're hosting next Thursday night in Tunbridge Wells.

And worse: turns out you're not the only one trying to get that person to click. The moment a friend or a business prospect swipes open their phone, checks their inbox or pops online to surf the web, there are loads of people shouting at the person to click on something else.

That's why, in a commercial world that increasingly takes place online, it is crucially important you embrace *the art of the click*.

Let me tell you right now: whatever business you might be in, to succeed in today's online marketplace, you must learn what it takes to write in a way that makes your prospects engage with you. Whether you're a marketer tasked with finding new prospects, a copywriter charged with monetising existing clients, or an entrepreneur running the whole shebang and you desperately need to boost your bottom line… you must learn what makes people click.

Good news is, you're in the right place. This book is *entirely* concerned with understanding what makes people click and throughout the following pages I will share with you different ways to write in a way that makes more people do so.

I assume no previous knowledge of copywriting, marketing or jujitsu. Actually, any prior knowledge of jujitsu would be pretty irrelevant here. Forget that. But definitely don't worry if you're not much of a whiz when it comes to marketing or copywriting right now *(you will be by the end of this book)*.

The way I see it is you might have picked up this book hoping to find ways to make more people click the 'Buy Now' button on your Etsy account. That's cool and I'll hopefully reveal how you can sell more of those cool little trinkets. You might have bought this book looking for tips on how to get more people to click on the 'Send Me Your Report' button you've got on your sales page, telling people about the interesting work you've produced with a highly respected rental property expert. Not a problem: let's get more of those free reports sent.

Or it could be you've published a book yourself and you're wondering if there's a way to sell more copies. That's great too. What I have to share here will help. Whatever your motivation for reading this book, it's cool with me. I'm just going to show you how to get people to click on stuff. Or in other words: get them to take action.

How? Ah, well. Here's the thing. I'm going to do it by teaching you about something called direct-response copywriting. Hmm. Hold on a moment. That sounds bit more technical than perhaps you'd like it to. It sure as hell doesn't sound very cool. That's because it's not cool, at least not in the opinion of most people.

But it is effective. Very effective. *(And for the record, I think it's kind of cool too.)*

By mastering direct-response copywriting, over the years I've helped different people and different businesses make millions of pounds, dollars and euros.

It doesn't matter how lofty your ambitions are: a few hours reading this book might help you improve the current marketing your company is doing and get you a nice pay-rise, or it might help you write a full direct-response sales letter that goes on to sell out your seminar in Tunbridge Wells and transforms your fortunes completely. Either way, whatever happens, I've done my best to make reading through this book entertaining and, quite possibly, enjoyable. No promises, though.

First, the big question: what is direct-response copywriting?

We'll get to that in much more detail shortly. But on a very high concept level, just think about it: to click on something is to respond directly to a request. Makes sense, right? Yet it seems to me so much of what's written about marketing online today takes its influence from the waffly world of what's known as indirect-response marketing. Again, we'll get to definitions in a moment, but you probably know the score. I'm talking about the funky hipsters hastily setting up agencies – who's biggest office expense is the Segway no one really uses anymore – and who gush about how important 'brand awareness' is and whether they should use a tiger or a puma in the next Mercedes advert to intimate just how powerful the car is.

Or maybe it's their forebears, the smarmy Italian-suited *ad men*, whose expense accounts read like a festival line-up of celebrity chefs and whose agencies rely on big corporation accounts that are too big to care that their marketing budget is spent on a single, sloppy rebranding pitch that promises to bring said company into the modern age by italicising the logo.

Sorry. Slipped into rant-mode there. But as we'll get to in a moment, there's an inherent problem with that indirect-response world, especially when it comes to marketing in today's crowded online marketplace. And it's why, in this book, I want to take the time to introduce to you, and show you how to harness, the power of direct-response copywriting.

You'll be writing better copy in no time

We are teetering. On the cusp. Peering over the edge. Of what? *Your new life,* of course. OK. OK. Look, I know that sounds ridiculous and a bit dramatic, but to be completely honest, it's kind of true. Well, it can be true if you want it to be. Let's put it that way. You see, throughout this book, I'm going to get you up to speed on how to write successful direct-response copy to a standard where you can TRANSFORM your business. Whether you own that business, or if you're currently hidden away in the marketing department, working desperately to prove your worth, this book will help you learn how to use direct-response copywriting to make a difference.

Indeed, regardless of where you're at right now, the basic rules are the same: you're going to need to keep an open mind, listen to what I say and put in a little bit of practice. Don't worry, it's NOT going to be a hard slog – at least, there's no need for it to be that way. Rather, you just need to set some time aside now and again to practise the stuff I teach you in these very pages.

In return for your commitment of a few hours here and there, I promise to help you as best I can. I will share with you throughout this book my own experience and insight into the world of direct-response copywriting and reveal how you can harness its power for yourself. Bottom line is: by the time you finish this book, you'll posses enough direct-response knowledge to be able to persuade almost anyone to click on almost anything.

Sound good? I hope so, because there's a shed load of stuff I need to talk to you about and if we don't get a move on, we'll be wandering around this introduction all day. I don't want that – I want to get to the good stuff.

But before we do, we need to cover a couple of fundamental things first, like why you should learn direct-response copywriting at all? And why exactly is everyone so obsessed with 'getting the click' these days? In fact, before we get to the specific questions at hand, let me take a very short detour to talk about myself. *Booooo! I don't want to hear about you, Glenn. Get to the good stuff and show me how to write better copy.* I know, I know. The last thing you want to hear about right now is me, but I'm afraid it's important – for my own sake, if nothing else – that I just tell you a little bit about myself and how I got into direct-response copy.

Everyone's story is different

There is method behind the madness. Trust me. Indeed, my own story will hopefully allow you to better understand the answer to that key question: why learn direct-response copywriting?

You see, after finishing college and deciding I didn't need to learn anything else (I was a bit too arrogant in my youth), I skipped university and went straight into the harsh world of nine-to-five employment. I worked for the local council in North East Lincolnshire (then South Humberside), and after working my way through various sections – Education, Finance, Housing Benefits – I ended up working in auditing. I don't want to go into it too far, but basically, I was the guy who goes into various council departments (and schools), examines their accounts and the systems they have in place for running said department (or school) and makes recommendations on how to improve things.

In hindsight, it turned out to be a good way to learn how businesses work – but at the time, after quickly working my way up the pay scale I realised something. It was dull. Worse than that, it was limited. I could only ever become the boss. Then I'd have another boss. Then I'd become that boss and find myself under another boss.

Anyway, at that point, I didn't know the name of what I wanted. I just knew I wanted something different. I know now that what I wanted was freedom. Plain and simple. That's where I am now. All thanks to direct-response copywriting.

In fact, I write these particular few pages to you from an apartment in Paris… as a free man. If you've ever seen the film *Amelie* and remember the grocery store she visits each day – I'm sat across from there. Listening to music. Drinking wine. And writing to you. Tomorrow, I'll wake. Take a stroll to the patisserie for breakfast. Drop into my favourite bookshop and then write another chapter of this book. In the afternoon, I'll find a quiet café, order a bottle of wine and read. Sure, it's a great situation to be in. That's why I want to share my knowledge with you in this book.

Don't get me wrong: you might not have such grand ambitions. Perhaps you're just looking to write some better adverts for the company you're working for, or you're a business owner who wants to learn more about how to sell their product. That's cool. I just want you to understand the potential of learning more about direct-response copywriting. It can change everything.

It's good because you know when it's bad

I like that sentence...

It's good because you know when it's bad.

Really, it sums up why I think direct-response copywriting is such a great skill to learn. And it's why I believe it's one of the best ways to transform the fortunes of any business. You see, direct-response copywriting is all about results. And because the results are immediate and easily measurable, it means you can quickly change your copy to be stronger so you get more clicks and achieve better results.

But I'm jumping ahead of myself a little here.

First, to make sure we're on the same page, let's just define a couple of important words. I mean, we've got this word 'copywriting' – what's that mean? Simple answer (for now) is that it's writing to sell. 'Copy' is any bit of writing that you come across that is being used to encourage someone to take some kind of action (usually it's an action that involves a monetary transaction of some kind).

That's the easy bit. The phrase 'direct-response' is a little more involved. To explain what it means, let me tell you a quick story...

Once upon a time, direct-response copywriting was considered 'the Don' of copywriting. Not the Don Draper. You see, Don Draper – the famous fictional copywriter from the TV series *Mad Men* – is an indirect-response man. He writes copy that's designed to briefly get your attention and then force the product to linger in your mind. And, if it's good indirect-response copy, it'll linger long enough to still be there when you're in the supermarket or on the high street and said product is sparkling before you, waiting to be bought. That's indirect-response copy – the action is delayed.

Direct-response copywriting is more – well, it's more direct. It is copy designed to lead the reader to a buying decision there and then, in that very moment. With direct-response copywriting – the action is immediate.

Now, I mention Don Draper for a reason. The TV series *Mad Men* was loosely based on the roaring trade the ad men of the 1960s enjoyed – specifically ad men like David Ogilvy. Ah, the name of god: David Ogilvy.

Yup, when it comes to copywriting, this guy always gets mentioned. And fair play to him: he was a bloody clever man. We'll come across him quite a lot during this book. (We should also give kudos to great copywriters such as Claude Hopkins, Eugene Schwartz and Gary Halbert, who have done amazing work for the world of copy.)

Ogilvy had hit after hit in the indirect-response world and defined a whole generation of copy. In fact, we're still not really out of it: his shadow looms large over a lot of the advertising copy you still see today. But why was he so good?

Why David Ogilvy loved direct-response

This is where direct-response copywriting comes back in. You see, David Ogilvy knew something very important: that to understand direct-response copywriting was to understand copywriting full stop. It's said he refused to employ any copywriter unless they'd spent at least two years studying direct-response copywriting. Ah, that's interesting. Why would he say that? Here's why:

> Direct-response copywriting is easily testable; indirect-response copywriting is not.

This is a great advantage for direct-response copy. And, as I say, it's what makes it such a good skill to learn. The fact that you have the ability to test variables in a controlled situation means you can work out what influences people to click on things and make a buying decision much quicker (and usually much cheaper) than you can with indirect-response copy.

Take a piece of indirect-copy – let's say a Coca-Cola advert featuring some polar bears having a lark. You run a print campaign in a national paper for two weeks. Immediately you don't know what the effect is. You hope that people notice the advert in the first place and then you hope that the thought of enjoying a coke lingers in their mind long enough to actually buy one when they're in the shop.

Two weeks later, you know sales of Coca-Cola have gone up, but is it because of the polar bears? Or is it because of something else? Who knows? Sure, you can try to measure the effect the advert has by featuring a website link, or by cancelling any other campaigns that might be running, or by comparing sales to the campaign last year. But let's face it, that's all a bit vague.

Instead, let's take a piece of direct-response copy. And just to show I'm not cheating here, we'll say it's for the same product – a can of Coca-Cola. This time you run an advert in the national paper that offers a coupon to the reader to get one free can with the next can he or she buys. Ignore for the minute that a free can is a better incentive than a polar bear frolicking – what's important here is the ability to test response. You see, now you can get an immediate response to your advert – people will respond or they won't. Fact. You'll know soon enough if the advert works or not.

And here's where it gets really good…

You can now run two adverts against each other. Hell, you can even run one advert with a picture of a polar bear offering a free can if you like and see if it works better than a bold headline telling you to 'Claim Your Free Coke'.

The point is, because the reader must now take immediate action, you can much better measure the reader's reaction to different variables. Quite simply: you can improve your copy based on facts, not just what a client thinks "would be cool". Ogilvy knew this. "Never stop testing, and your advertising will never stop improving," he said.

The ability to test variables in a piece of copy is enormously powerful and that is why a good understanding of direct-response copywriting is such a highly valued skill. It's why, once you've gone through this book with me, you'll be able to write much better copy to sell your products and services. It pays to remember that at its heart, copywriting is essentially just passing a message on. And direct-response means you're just looking to make sure the message gets where it needs to go and is put into action.

No experience needed

I don't know where you are with your life at the moment. You might already be on your way to becoming a copywriter and you're looking for some extra guidance… a path to follow that will make sure you know what you're talking about. Or you might be brand new to this… you may have seen the blurb for this book and got excited by the thought of developing a skill that could help you further your job as a marketer or designer. It may be you're a jack-of-all-trades entrepreneur and you want to master direct-response copywriting so you can take over the world.

The good news is, whoever you are, whatever your background, and no matter what your expectations are, I think I can help. You see, in this book – *even if you are already a relatively accomplished writer* – I'm going to ask you to forget everything you think you know. We need to start with a clean slate.

Believe me, you're not the first to go through this process – I've trained numerous people who came to me with wildly different levels of experience. From people who had never even heard of copywriting, to old pros who wanted to learn my own techniques after seeing me have such great success with them. Please don't worry if you don't consider yourself an accomplished writer at the moment – you don't need to be. You just need to be sure that you can pass on a message.

Are you ready? Are you sitting comfortably? Are you excited? I hope so, because in the first few chapters of this book we're going to cover a lot of important concepts that will form the foundation of your understanding and your ability to write direct-response copy.

Please, please, PLEASE do not skip over anything. Some of the things I ask you to do will sound like hard work. But they're not. It's more a rite of passage – it's something every accomplished independent direct-response copywriter must go through. And so must you.

One other thing you should know about this book

One of my old copywriting mentors was a bit of a crazy figure in the industry. Having proved himself by writing successful copy for a number of years, he pretty much came and went as he pleased.

He technically had a desk next to mine, but he hardly ever used it. I'd sit there waiting for him to arrive, hoping he'd give me some kind of direction or insight into how to write copy. Sometimes I'd wait for days. Then he'd come along and sit down with a pile of books – that had nothing to do with copywriting – and randomly suggest a cheeky pint at the local boozer. Naturally, I went along.

But I couldn't help wonder when the training was going to start. I'm not sure it ever did. Not in any structured way. I mostly learned from reading his work, asking the odd question when I could and generally doing my own research into things – reading on the web, asking other people around the office what was going on, and listening to other mentors. In this way, I started to develop as my career progressed.

But still, my first *training,* so to speak, came in this ad hoc and seemingly random way. And I don't think that was necessarily a bad thing.

That's why throughout this whole book, expect the unexpected. Obviously, I've gone to great pains to break this book down into manageable pieces that will ensure you don't blow your mind in one go, or have you running ahead before you can walk… there's an inherent structure to it, kind of. I think that's good as it allows us to measure where we are and make sure we're on the same page. But I also want to leave room for the unexpected. I want to have the scope to be as random in teaching you how to develop this skill as that first mentor was with me.

Don't worry – I won't be doing anything too drastic or random, but I will divert sometimes and go off about things that seem to be irrelevant. But they won't be – eventually you'll see the method behind my madness. I hope that's OK.

Also, I should point out one thing I will make sure I don't inherit from that old mentor. When you need to ask a question – I'll be there to answer it. I fully expect you to have various questions and queries as you progress through the book and I want you to feel happy that at any time you can email me and I'll do my best to answer you and clear up the problem as soon as possible. If you want to get hold of me, you can email me any time at **allgoodcopy@gmail.com** and simply mark the subject line with 'The Art of the Click' – that way I'll see it's from you and know to treat it as a priority.

Top Tip

When it comes to direct-response copywriting, you need to make sure that the words you use are simple and easy to understand. Yet, in English lessons at school, we're often encouraged to write as pretentiously as possible, using difficult words that get high marks in essays, but which would never be understood by the average reader. Even if you're already an accomplished writer with a huge vocabulary – please don't try to use it. You need to unlearn your fancy words and start writing how you speak.

Part One

Before You Write A Word

Chapter One
All Great Copywriters Start Here

> *"Good advertising does not just circulate information."*
> — **Leo Burnett**

There are too many like Jimmy in advertising

Jimmy's just started as a junior copywriter at a big information publisher, which mainly publishes financial advice. Jimmy doesn't know anything about copywriting. He did media studies at university, but has since struggled to find work. He's always enjoyed telling stories, but isn't much of writer. Still, he managed to fluke his way through an interview and now he's here in the office looking around, wondering what to do.

He's been told to write two short messages. He's been given the contents of the message and he's been told whom the message is for. He just needs to write it out. Each message is about 500 words. He does his best and hands in the two messages to his boss, who looks at the messages and asks, not politely, "What's this?" Jimmy's not sure what to say. He did what he was told. He's had no training and doesn't really understand why he was doing what he was doing. He just did it. The boss – who's a little stupid – thinks Jimmy is a flake and has already resolved to sack him; just as soon he's got more evidence of his shortcomings.

Poor Jimmy. Of course, we know that Jimmy has done nothing wrong – he was told to write two short messages, he was told what to write and he carried out his task accordingly. At no point was he asked to understand why he was doing what he was doing. And at no point was he given the opportunity to do so. It's not his fault his boss is stupid. It plays out that Jimmy spends three months trying to understand what his boss really wants, until finally he's sacked, just at the point he's started to understand the job he's tasked with.

Jimmy's is a sad story, but it's one that happens all too often – especially in the world of direct-response copywriting. Sadly I've seen too many like Jimmy go through the system – and worse, I've seen too many bosses like that. Yet this is how most people attempt to learn direct-response copy – writing short messages first, without really understanding why. They don't see the bigger picture. Sure, some grow into half decent writers, but their vision is tunnelled. They'll never be *truly* successful.

That's not good. And it's not what I want for you. This is why I changed the way I teach copywriters.

The champagne fountain of good copy

You know those slightly tacky champagne fountains you see, where there are layers upon layers of glasses on top of each other until you reach a single glass at the top? And then you pour the champagne into that one glass and the sparkling goodness flows down from the single glass, filling all the glasses beneath it?

That's how this will be.

You see, we're going to start with learning about *long copy*, and everything else will flow from there, to make learning how to write other types of copy a lot easier.

Jimmy's problem was that he didn't know that the two small messages he was being asked to write were part of a much longer message. If he had known that, he would have been able to write the smaller messages more easily and to a standard that his idiot boss was happy with.

But hold on one second. What is long copy? Ah. Yes. I'm getting ahead of myself again. We need to do a little bit of defining before we go any further. So, *long copy* – what do I mean by that?

The key characters in direct-response

Depending on whom you speak to, you get all sorts of definitions for things in the world of direct-response copywriting. It can seem daunting when you're starting out, but don't worry – these things become second nature after a while. Indeed, as you work your way through this book, all this jargon will slowly but surely work its way into your brain. The best thing I think we can do is to quickly run through a few of the main characters in direct-response copywriting and give you a brief explanation of what they are.

The first thing I need to introduce you to is the long copy sales letter.

The long copy sales letter

Usually between 20 and 50 pages, the long copy sales letter is the pinnacle of direct-response copywriting.

In the coming pages of this book, I'm going to teach you how these letters work. I'm going to break it down into easy to understand pieces so that you'll be able to follow my lead and write your own long copy sales letters. Of course you might never want or need to write a long copy sales letter, but by understanding how they work, you'll be able to write much stronger copy for any medium, be it a pay-per-click (PPC) advert, a Facebook post, or an off-the-page advert.

For now, what you need to know is that the long copy sales letter has one single function – to persuade the reader to take immediate action by purchasing the product or service you're writing the letter about. That's it.

Now that might seem like common sense, but please never forget that the one overriding function of a long copy sales letter is to persuade the reader to buy immediately. When we get deeper into this book, you'll see that people get awfully elaborate about the purpose of different bits of copy. I don't want you to get confused. Stick with me and set this fact to memory:

The function of a long copy sales letter is to persuade the reader to take immediate action.

On the jargon side of things, you'll sometimes hear a long copy sales letter referred to as a sales promotion, a promo, a package, or a pack. These are all essentially the same thing.

Email copy

Remember Jimmy? This is what he was asked to write: the two short messages. You see, to get people to read a long copy sales letter, you need to write a piece of copy that directs them to it. Jimmy's problem was that he didn't understand his messages were meant to lead to a long copy sales letter.

There are many names for the emails you send to people to get them to read a long copy sales letter. Some people call them endorsements (in the sense that you're endorsing the sales letter), others call them lift notes (this goes back to the days of direct mail), and others simply refer to them as email copy.

The one single aim of email copy in this case is to get the reader to arrive at the sales letter in the right mood to read it. We'll come back to this in another part of the book; there's a lot to talk about here.

Auto-responder copy

This is a phrase you hear a lot as a direct-response copywriter – but all it really means is a number of pieces of email copy delivered in succession, automatically. Auto-responder series are used by internet marketers to avoid having to contact new readers manually: you can set up a series of emails that new readers will receive in order, which are aimed to get them to read your long copy sales letters.

Squeeze pages

Also called landing pages, squeeze pages are kind of like very short, sales letters. They're usually one or two pages long and invite a reader to enter their email address to receive more information about a product or service.

Content

This is any article or blog post that is related to the overall marketing campaign. People don't often consider things like articles and blog posts as part of direct-response copywriting. Some people elevate them to their own niche altogether and so we hear silly phrases like "content marketing". Content marketing isn't a thing. All marketing involves content. When it comes to direct response copywriting, I consider any article or blog post that is written around the same theme as the copy you're working on to be part of the overall copy project. If you can begin to sow the seeds of your copy in the content, you're on to a winner.

For now, those are the main elements of copy you need to know about. There are order forms and order confirmations and welcome letters and stuff like that, but it's not too important that you know about them just yet. You see, I return to my point. Everything about direct-response copywriting – especially when it comes to learning about it – comes back to long copy sales letters.

Every persuasion technique that you need in a piece of email copy, you will use in a long copy sales letter. Every psychological tool you use in a squeeze page will also be used in a long copy sales letter. Every principle of repetition that you understand for auto-responder copy will be something you've learnt studying long copy sales letters.

This is why I'm going to teach you everything I know about long copy sales letters. Because after we've done that, everything else is much, much easier. Sure, it might seem like were only focusing on one format – or going a bit too slow for your liking. But trust me, when you've finished this book, and when you find yourself already miles ahead of the competition, you'll thank me.

I hope you enjoy reading

Before we move on, I want you to take some time to read a long copy sales letter in full. It won't take you long – probably about 30 minutes in all. And don't worry too much about trying to work out why what's written has been written, or how the message has been put together. I just want you to read. This first stage of learning about direct-response copy should be pretty organic. Don't rush. Instead, I want you to let things sink in, to trust your brain and its ability to digest information for you, without you consciously realising you're doing it.

If possible, change your surroundings to read the letter. Go to the garden, or lay on the bed. Just find somewhere comfortable where you won't be disturbed and read. The letter is one I wrote many years ago, but it was very successful and contains within it a lot of elements that all good copy should have. It's by no means a perfect piece, but having generated thousands in sales, it's a good starting point.

The sales letter itself is for a copywriting guide I wrote many years ago that aims to share a few secrets with the reader. Don't worry too much about the ins and outs of the letter – that's not what this is about. Just read it and then we'll continue.

Once you've read the sales letter, then we can move on to the next part of the journey. But please, ensure you DO read the letter first. If you skip straight to the next part, you'll be missing out on something very important.

While you read the letter – let's pause for a moment. I'll go make myself a cup of tea and we'll take this up again in a minute. OK?

Direct-response copywriting expert, Glenn Fisher, reveals more than 20 tried and tested techniques for improving your sales copy, starting with...

The simple secret to writing copy that sells

Whether you're working on copy for a sales letter, a website or an 'off the page' advert – the advice I'll share with you will help to make it more effective

In fact, I'd like to arrange a **one-to-one copy critique** with you so we can discuss how to improve a specific piece of copy you're working on

But first, there's a **myth about copywriting** and how people address potential customers that I'd like to dispel...

Fellow Marketer and Copywriter,

People think only *difficult* writing is good writing.

For years we study the classics, we build our vocabulary, we learn how to craft our sentences and paragraphs.

All through this period there is an unspoken suggestion – if you don't understand what you're reading, it's your fault. It's not that the book is difficult to understand, it's that YOU are too dumb to understand it.

So you read more, you learn more, you waste your time working through impossible literature that means nothing to you.

I've done it.

He's done it. *(I'm talking about the imaginary guy sat next to me)*

And if you're a writer of any kind, you've probably done it too.

Don't worry. It happens.

Only problem is, if you decide after all this that you're going to work in advertising – you're buggered.

The first thing I had beaten out of me – and the first thing I beat out of any trainee copywriter – is the misapprehension that only difficult writing is good writing.

The crappy flowery language that 'writers-to-be' adopt in their early days *(to prove themselves as 'an artist')* needs slapping down. In fact, it needs to be slapped down, taken outside and then stamped on repeatedly until it resembles a Jackson Pollock painting.

When you're hoping to sell something to someone who doesn't really want to be sold to, you need to speak as simply and as directly as possible. You need to write as though you're explaining it to a mate.

Be casual. Be long-winded if you need to be. But be natural.

Because if you can be yourself in your writing, your message – whatever it may be – WILL shine through, trust me.

Whether you're a copywriter or a marketer, when it comes to writing sales copy, the fact is...

You write to sell.

And the more you sell; the more money YOU make.

It figures, right?

That's why **it is so important** that your copywriting is as effective as it can be.

Hell, it doesn't matter if you're writing copy for your own products, or you're writing copy for somebody else's...

The more effective YOUR copy, the more YOU get paid.

That's why, right now, not only would I like to arrange a one-to-one copy critique, I'm going to share more than 20 quick and simple techniques that I have personally used to at least double the conversion of my own writing and sell a hell of a lot more.

In fact, I'm not bragging, but these very tactics have helped me write copy that has made **over £10 million**, selling everything from online marketing courses to Elvis' hair.

- **Each technique has been tested and PROVEN to increase conversion.**

- **Each technique is simple to understand and easy to apply to ANY sales copy, regardless of what product or service you might be selling.**

- **And each technique can be used over and over again to boost the conversion of your copy whenever you need it.**

Whatever level you are at as a copywriter, you'll be able to use these **tried and tested techniques** to improve your copywriting and make a ton more sales.

Seriously.

Even if you have already written copy that has sold millions, you'll still discover a number of techniques that you have **NOT** tried before... and they could very easily **make your copy EVEN MORE effective**.

And remember...

The more effective YOUR copy, the more YOU get paid.

Of course, if you ARE an experienced copywriter, you know that, right?

You *already* realise how important it is to collect as much expert insight as you can.

And hey, if you're new to copywriting...

Well, I'm sure you understand that too. I'm sure you understand that studying the techniques of fellow writers who have had great success with their own sales writing is ESSENTIAL to your success as a copywriter.

The good news is that the techniques you'll discover today will give you **new skills and insight** to help you write copy that will sell far more than you ever realised you could – no matter what copywriting experience you have.

Just like Blanca here, who wrote to report:

Write Better Copy is a life jacket for those who are dipping their toe into the wild marketing waters and sinking. When I started to study copywriting, I desperately needed the right tool to tidy all the information I was receiving in my mind. I found it in Write Better Copy.

Blanca, Journalist and Copywriter

And, of course, during our one-to-one copy critique (I'll explain how it'll work in a moment) we can discuss these ideas further so that you can take your copywriting to a whole new level.

Personally, I have seen these tactics **multiply conversion four or even FIVE times** on more than one occasion.

And just think about how that could change your copy...

There's no need to start from scratch – just take a few minutes to tweak your existing sales material and you could make twice as many sales

Best of it is, applying just a handful of these techniques could not only increase the *conversion* of your current copy...

They could do it INSTANTLY.

You see, to take full advantage of these **simple** and **straight-forward** techniques, you only need you to make a few quick tweaks to your *current* copy!

There's absolutely NO need to rewrite everything you've already done.

I mean, you've undoubtedly put a lot of hard work into your copy, right? The last thing you want to do is start again.

Before we do anything then, I just want to help you make the most of what you've already got.

So, just pick **one or two** of the techniques I'll share with you today...

Take **a couple minutes to tweak** your current copy accordingly...

And then just get it in front of customers and **let your new, super-charged copy do its work.**

Hey, if you want to test the new version against the old version, go for it.

In fact, you probably should so you can see exactly how much my advice helps you.

But to be open with you, I really am **100% convinced** that you'll discover that any copy you tweak using these techniques will outperform your existing copy.

I mean, you'll discover:

- **The one thing you MUST do before you write a single word of copy – whether it's a sales letter, a PPC advert or a website banner, you need to make sure you consider this before even putting pen to paper...**

- **A way of thinking about what you're selling that will help you write breakthrough headlines – approaching copy like this will not only make more sales, it will free up your time to enjoy the money you make from copywriting...**

- **The right way to end your copy that will increase the amount of sales you make and change the mind of anyone who was previously sceptical – this is one of the biggest mistakes made in copywriting and you can avoid it...**

- **An 'inception trick' you can apply to a few sentences in your copy that will force an idea into the mind of your reader without them even realising it – you shouldn't overuse this, but when you do use it, it'll make your copy irresistible...**

- **How to use an experimental writing technique that will not only make your reader WANT to buy the product or service you're selling, they will actually learn from you and want to thank you for selling it to them...**

- **How to properly deal with an author's image in a way that is fundamental to the success of ANY sales letter - even the best copywriters in the business get this wrong and damage their conversion because of it...**

- **The one thing I insist on doing with every single product or service I write copy for - this one factor alone contributes more to the success of my own copywriting than anything else I've ever learned...**

- **How adding a distinctive 'SympAck' section to a failing promotion could transform it into a huge sales success - most people don't do this, but it could be the difference between a breakthrough and a complete flop...**

- **Why you should never use more than twelve words for one key element of your sales promotion (and it's not the headline) - this is so simple, but when you see how it works you'll always do it without fail.**

I don't know which you'll use first, but whichever one it is, you can be sure the result will be the same...

Your copy WILL be more effective.

And hey, don't get me wrong...

If you decide that the tried and tested techniques that I'd like to share with you today aren't going to help you increase the conversion of your current copy...

That's fair enough.

In fact, even though I am 100% convinced that these WILL help you, if you get hold of a copy of the guide I've put together and decide in the next 60 days that it's not going to help you...

You can get a **full** and **complete refund**.

I won't hold it against you or make you jump through any hoops...

Just let me know and you'll get the cost of the guide right back.

I don't want you to have to take **ANY** risk here. Why should you?

I just want to share these ideas with you so they can make a difference to your copy.

Actually, that's an important point...

Not only can you make your current promotions more effective, you'll discover simple 'copy workouts' that you can use to help teach yourself

Of course, it's up to you how you play it...

You could just read through each of the different ideas you'll discover today and put them into action without giving it a second thought.

That's fine.

But because **I'm a copywriter like you**, I understand that it is much more valuable to learn WHY one certain copy technique increases conversion and another doesn't.

It took me years to figure out what works and what doesn't...

Not to mention a hell of a lot of money spent on seminars, flights around the world and more 'how to' books than I care to recall.

But by **studying under copywriting legends** like *Bill Bonner, Michael Masterson* and *John Forde* and dissecting the teachings of past masters like *Claude Hopkins, Eugene Schwartz* and *Gary Halbert*...

I realised something very simple but very fundamental.

The key to truly improving your skills as a copywriter is practice.

You simply can't beat putting ideas and concepts into actual, real-life, 'pen to paper' practice. I know that doesn't sound 'sexy' and it sure as hell doesn't sound like fun... but it's not actually all bad and it will make you more money in the long-run.

That is a simple fact.

That's why, with each of the tried and tested **conversion booster tactics** I've laid out in this guide, I've also included a simple '**copy workout**' that you can do whenever you want to flex your muscles and improve your own copywriting abilities.

Not only have I used these workouts to help hone my own copywriting skills...

These very same exercises have been used to train very successful copywriters working in the business today and have helped them to **bank a lot more money than they ever thought they would ever make.**

Together with the techniques I'll share with you, these 'copy workouts' will enable you to constantly improve your copy.

And remember, you can checkout the workouts and test each of the tactics over the next 60 days and if you're not *completely and utterly* confident that they will help you write better copy...

You can get a full refund.

No questions asked.

You'll have an entire 60 days to read through everything and make your own fully-informed decision.

There's no catch. I'm just making a simple offer to share the techniques that **I have personally used to generate over £10 million in sales**.

Look... all these ideas will help you write better copy.

And as I said before, it doesn't matter if you're writing copy for your own products and services, or you're writing copy for somebody else's...

The more effective your copy, the more you get paid.

That's why I'd like to share these quick and simple **conversion-boosting techniques** that I have personally used to at least double the conversion of my own writing and sell much, much more.

But the fact of the matter is: this is **just the start** of us sharing ideas.

COPY BOOSTER BONUS #1:
You'll receive access to an exclusive video series revealing my personal methods for fixing broken copy

This is a first...

In fact, there is simply no other way you can get access to this EXCLUSIVE video series.

But when you get hold of the techniques I'd like to share with you today, I will give you unlimited access to the series at no extra cost.

The only thing I do ask is that you **keep these methods to yourself.**

You see, in each video I reveal one of *my own personal techniques* for examining sales copy that isn't performing as well as it should be and fixing the problem.

You'll discover:

- **How the 'Three Strike Strategy' works and how it can help you rid your copy of boring sections that turn off your readers and lose you sales – you'll be able to put this simple strategy into practice straight away on all your current copy...**

- **What to do when you finish a sales letter to view it from the reader's point of view with absolutely no bias – you'll need to do this when no-one is watching or else you'll look strange, but I GUARANTEE it will improve your writing...**

- **The four things you need to check of any headline to make sure it grabs a reader's attention so that they simply HAVE to read it – this has helped me turn failed promotions into consistent profit makers time and time again...**

As soon as you pop your details in today, I'll direct you to an exclusive members area where you can watch the videos whenever you want to and as many times as you want to.

But that's not the only bonus you'll receive today...

COPY BOOSTER BONUS #2:
Get a promotion of your choice personally reviewed by me – you'll get specific and tailored advice on how you can improve it

This would normally cost you around £1,000...

And even then, I only usually do this for a **very select group** of close copywriting friends.

But because I want to help you today as best as I can...

And because, as I say, I really want this to be just the start of our relationship...

When you get hold of the guide I've put together for you full of these incredibly effective direct response techniques, you'll also receive a **one-on-one, personal email consultation**.

I will personally critique the promotion of your choice – whether it's a new one you're working on, or it's one that isn't working so well and you need to improve it – and give you **specific and tailored advice** on how to tweak it so that it makes more sales.

This is about me and you working out how to make your copy stronger...

Together.

Just like I've worked with copywriters who have gone on to write breakthrough sales promotions that have grossed thousands and thousands of pounds...

I'll be working with YOU to make sure your promotion works as best as it can do.

As soon as you get your details down today... along with access to the special member's area where you'll be able to watch the EXCLUSIVE video tutorials (which I insist you get for no extra charge)...

You'll also receive details of where to send the promotion you'd like to work on with me so that we can get right on it.

Actually though, as a brief aside, you're probably wondering why I'm in a position to be showing anyone how to improve their copywriting in the first place?

Well...

Everything I've learned about copywriting comes from strict direct-response tests that prove one thing works better than another

To be completely honest, I don't want to talk about myself too much...

Because this is all about helping **YOU**.

But I realise that one of the biggest objections I would have if someone was telling me they knew how to improve their copywriting is: why do you know any more than me?

To be fair, if I've learned one thing in life, it's that I don't know much...

But I do seem to know a bit about copywriting and I have **one advantage** over most...

Everything I have discovered is PROVEN by testing.

You see, one of my biggest clients is The Agora, who are one of the biggest information publishers in the world. You might have heard of them.

If not, the company was started by a legendary copywriter in his own right, Bill Bonner, along with another legendary copywriter called Mark Ford (who you might better know by his pen name: Michael Masterson).

Not only have I been lucky enough to be taught by Bill and Mark personally, but because of the sheer size of The

Agora's customer database, I have been able to **split-test my own copy to an incredible degree**.

Of course, a lot of the **conversion-boosting techniques** I've discovered were initially based on my own gut instinct, but through *rigorous* testing I've been able to analyse copy like few other copywriters have the opportunity to do.

Especially on such a scale.

So while I could go on about all the success I've personally had as a copywriter – *it's taken me around the world to many places I wouldn't have ever have been otherwise* – that's NOT really what qualifies me to share these ideas with you...

What *really counts* is that **everything** I'll share with you has been tested and proven to increase response.

So, it's not so much *me* teaching you anything.

What will be informing **your increased success** are the reactions of the very customers you'll be selling more to.

But we were talking about the copy boosting bonuses you'll receive today...

COPY BOOSTER BONUS #3:
You'll receive regular ongoing insight and advice about how to write better copy – and it won't cost you a penny...

So, as well as getting your hands on more than **20 techniques to improve your direct response copy**...

As well as receiving access to the **EXCLUSIVE video tutorials**...

And as well as being able to **work one-on-one with me** to improve a sales promotion of your choice...

You'll ALSO get my weekly e-letter, which is entirely dedicated to helping you learn how to write better copy.

In each issue of the e-letter you'll discover one important idea that you can put into action to **increase how effective your copywriting is** so that you can make more sales and make more money.

And hopefully, you'll have fun reading it too. I mean, the whole aim of the e-letter is to be informative but entertaining at the same time.

In recent issues I've shared with readers:

- **How sleeping with your readers could actually improve your copywriting – don't worry, this isn't as dangerous, or as perverted as it sounds... but it really could help you when it comes to writing your next breakthrough promotion...**

- **What Woody Allen can teach you about copywriting – if you only spend your time reading textbooks written by hacks who worked for some ad agency once upon a time, you'll get nowhere. You can find inspiration for copy from the strangest people...**

- **Why it is so important to repeat yourself even when you think you shouldn't – it's one of the most contentious points in professional copywriting and online marketing, but readers discovered why it sometimes pays to go against the grain...**

And here's the best thing...

Even if you decide that the guide isn't for you and it's not going to help you improve your copywriting...

Not only will you **still** be able to get access to the video tutorials...

Not only will you **still** be able to receive my weekly e-letter...

I will **STILL** provide you with a one-on-one copy review to help you improve a promotion of your choice.

You can get hold of the guide today, take a look over it and decide it's just not right for you and claim a refund and you'll still get all three of these excellent copy booster bonuses.

Of course, I don't think you'll want to refund.

In fact, I think you'll probably be thinking **you have pulled a swift one on me** anyway because you'll be getting so much value for so little.

You see, to download a copy of the guide – that I've simply called **Write Better Copy** – and discover more than 20 quick and simple conversion-boosting techniques that I have personally used to at least double the conversion of my own writing and sell much, much more...

To get exclusive access – *access that you genuinely can't get anywhere else* – to a special **series of tutorial videos** in which I'll show you my own techniques for fixing sales copy that doesn't work...

To receive **a one-on-one, personalised copy review** by email, in which we will work together to improve the sales promotion of your choice...

And to start receiving a copy of my personal weekly e-letter delivered directly to your inbox full of copywriting insight and advice...

All you'll pay today is **just £19.95 or $30.98 if you're in the US**.

That is a one-off cost...

There are absolutely no hidden charges...

And you can pay securely and with 100% confidence through Clickbank, using whichever currency you prefer.

Really, to receive the conversion booster techniques... the exclusive tutorial videos... the one-on-one copy review... and the weekly e-letter...

It will cost you a small, one-off payment of just £19.95 or $30.98 if you're in the US.

Considering that putting just ONE of the conversion booster tactics into action could more than double the conversion of your current sales promotion, that's nothing.

But when you think about how many different **conversion-boosting techniques** you'll discover today and how much of an effect they could have on your copywriting...

I hope you'll consider it a wise purchase.

And I mean, that's not even considering how much it would cost you to hire me to go through a sales promotion with you and give you specific, tailored advice on how to improve it.

Even so...

You'll have an entire 60 days to put all this to the test to see first hand how it helps you improve your copy and make more sales

Look, I really wanted to over-deliver here...

And hopefully, you'll think I have.

But look...

If you decide to give this a shot today to see how these **proven techniques** could help you to improve your copy...

To have a watch of the **exclusive tutorial videos**...

And to even go through the **one-on-one review** process with me...

Your money *still* won't be committed in any way.

You see, at ANY time during the next 60 days you can request a refund and you'll be paid back your £19.95 or $30.98 if you're in the US, without me raising a single objection.

Really: if you decide this isn't for you at any point over the next two months, you can get a **full** and **complete** refund, with no questions asked.

I am of the firm belief that if this isn't for you, **you shouldn't have to pay for it**. As I say, you can still have unrestricted access to the videos, you can still get a one-on-one copy review with me by email and you can still continue to receive my weekly e-letter...

Consider it thanks for at least giving this a go because I really do respect anyone who actively seeks to improve their skill set like you are doing right now.

BRAND NEW COPY BOOSTER BONUS: A free copy of my five-star rated e-book, which reveals 10 rules every direct response copywriter should follow when starting out

As I say, I really want to provide you with as much advice and insight as I can and help you become a more successful copywriter...

So, if you get hold of **Write Better Copy** today, you'll also be able to download a copy of **Buy This Now: A Beginner's Guide to Direct-Response Copywriting**.

In this easy and entertaining book you'll discover ten simple things that you can always do to make sure your copy stands out above the crowd.

From understanding the importance of a varied vocabulary to learning how to swallow your creative pride, **Buy This Now** will give you the perfect stepping stone to a long and successful career as a direct-response copywriter.

In fact, you can see here just how useful people have found it:

> *This is definitely my go-to resource for direct response copywriting. Glenn's engaging writing style makes you want to read to the end in one go. Even his sentence construction made me understand how direct response advertising works. If you have any inclination to make money with copywriting, download this book now!*

Elizabeth, Copywriter

> *Absolutely cracking book. Well written (obviously) and plenty of `highlight' worthy nuggets of wisdom. This book will undoubtedly be on the "need to re-read that again" list!*

Matt R, Copywriter

> *I am about to launch a website with a direct response letter to increase sales for my latest book. Man o man am I glad I found this. I have read extensively on the*

art of copywriting, but I got to say this gem is one of the best. He is not only practiced and a professional copywriter but quite literary and funny. How refreshing to find someone who connects on so many levels.

The Happy Hombre, Entrepreneur and Copywriter

When it comes down to it then, it's pretty simple...

Right now, I'd like to share more than 20 quick and simple **conversion booster tactics** that I have personally used to at least double the conversion of my own writing and sell much, *much* more...

And if over the next 60 days you don't find them useful, you can get your money back.

In addition to the guide itself, you'll also receive access to my exclusive video mini-series, you'll get a one-on-one copy critique, you'll get my regular advice emails...

AND you'll get a free copy of *Buy This Now*.

Thinking about it like that hopefully makes you realise that you really can't lose ANYTHING by giving this a go...

In fact, considering all you'll get just for giving it a go, then it'd be a bit silly to ignore this opportunity now. But that's **YOUR** choice to make.

For my part, I hope that you understand that this is *just the first stage of the relationship we've started today* and I hope that we'll be able to share ideas more and more over the coming weeks and months...

And it's important to remember that everything that I want to share with you today is not made up or hypothesis... these are **tips, techniques and even a few tricks** that I have *personally* used to write better copy.

You know better than anyone that the more effective your copy, the more you get paid.

So, to make your copy more effective today...

Just click the link here or the 'Order Now' button below to get your copy of *Write Better Copy* for just £19.95 or $30.98 if you're in the US.

ORDER NOW

Best Wishes,

Glenn Fisher

Glenn Fisher
Direct Response Copywriter
Author of *Write Better Copy*

P.S. Remember, not only will you be able to download your copy of ***Writer Better Copy*** as soon as you've got your details down today...

You'll also get immediate access to the **exclusive video tutorials** I've put together for you...

And you'll be able to get in touch to arrange when we can sort out your **personalised one-on-one copy review** by email.

ORDER NOW

P.P.S. I haven't mentioned this until now, but there's also a special invitation in the guide itself, which will give you the opportunity to actually **get paid by me** for the copy you write.

I'll explain everything in the guide, but basically, if you're able to use the conversion booster tactics that you'll receive in a moment, you could end up receiving **royalty cheques** from me for years to come!

That's no joke.

It's a serious proposition that will hopefully mean we can take our professional relationship to a **mutually profitable** stage.

So, to take advantage of this incredible opportunity today for **just £19.95 or $30.98 if you're in the US...**

ORDER NOW

Finished reading? Good – and well done. Let's move on to the next chapter. Oh, and that was an excellent cup of tea by the way.

Top Tip

You should keep what's known as a *swipe file*. It's a file – though it could be a folder, a Word document or a dog that you've intricately tattooed – that records copy you've seen. I was going to say *good* copy. But really you should fill your swipe file with good **and** bad copy. Good copy so you can take inspiration for your own writing. Bad copy so you can make sure you avoid making the same mistakes. That's the aim of a swipe file: to inspire new writing, whilst avoiding old tired writing. The key to keeping a good piece of copy is not just storing the copy on file for the sake of it. You need to analyse each piece of copy in your file – using the insight you take from this book. You can then refer to these notes later when you consult your swipe file.

Chapter Two
The Importance of Rote Learning

"Happiness is the longing for repetition."

— Milan Kundera

A copywriter's rite of passage

When I first tell you about this technique, you might think I'm crazy. It's annoying. But it is easy. And it's one of the best ways to learn how to write great copy. Problem is, when people start out, they tend to be either too arrogant or too lazy to actually do this. It's a shame. Because every top copywriter I've ever spoken to remembers having done this, at least a few times. And the more I think about it – and the more I write myself – the more I realise how important this technique is.

Before you get down to the nitty-gritty of getting the click – like making headlines stronger, bringing out the benefits of a product, or introducing an irresistible offer – you'll much better spend your time doing this.

Doing what…?

Writing out good copy by hand. Boring, right? Maybe so, but trust me here. If you want to harness the power of direct-response copywriting, doing this will form the strongest foundation possible. You're in great company…

Ernest Hemingway. He's considered a pretty good writer, huh? And you've heard of Stephen King, right? He's knocked out a few bestsellers. Or maybe you prefer a bit of an alternative angle to your literature; a bit of JG Ballard, perhaps? Well, let me tell you. All three admit that when they were starting out in their writing careers they used to sit there and copy out – by hand – the work of other writers. And it's not just fiction writers who do this. As I say, all of the best copywriters I know have sat down and copied out sales promotions written by their peers.

In fact, I might go as far as to say you're not a proper direct-response copywriter unless you've written out by hand at least three different sales promotions. It sounds boring, monotonous and somewhat pointless, but please believe me that doing so will help you to write and review copy to a much a higher standard than you presently do.

Everything after will be so much easier. It's no big secret. And it isn't fancy. But it works. You probably know that learning something in this way is known as rote learning. And there's a ton of debate on how effective rote learning is. A lot of people are dismissive of it. But when it comes to writing direct-response copy, it will help. You see, by writing out a piece of copy over and over you'll start to pick up the style, the grammar, the sentence structure, the pacing. You'll start to get a feel for it.

Sure, you might not realise the reason why something is worded in a particular way – understanding that will come later – but you will understand how it is worded and how to emulate the wording. After writing out a good piece of long copy a few times, when it comes to writing something from scratch, you'll find it much easier. It will be a lot more natural.

Pick up a pen and write it out

This action point comes in two parts. The first part is essential and you really must do it if you're going to get the most out of this book and become a better copywriter.

The second part is an extension of the first part and isn't as essential, but I would encourage you to do it anyway as it will make you a stronger writer. It will help in the long run, trust me.

So, for starters, I'd like you to take the long copy sales letter you just read and copy it out by hand. Simple, eh? Again, I don't want you to be thinking too much at this stage. You've got to trust your brain – this first step on the journey is all very subconscious. Don't worry, in the coming chapters we'll be looking at some very technical things that will help you write better copy.

For now though, as I say, I just want you to copy that sales letter out by hand and that's all.

WARNING: Please keep hold of your handwritten version, as you will need it for another part of the book.

OK. That's part one of this particular action point covered. The second part requires you to do a little research...

Good artists copy, great artists steal

I'd like you to search for some more copy that's working well and copy that out by hand as well. If you're wondering what copy is working, it's pretty easy to spot. Basically, if you see the same promotion on a number of occasions, it's more than likely it's working well. To find examples of direct-response copy letters, see the Top Tip on page 49. Now, get hold of some copy and take the time to write it out. And after you've written it once... do it again. And then, if you really want to get good at this, do it again.

You don't have to do it all in one go. An hour here or there is fine. What's important is that you write it out exactly as it's written and repeat it as many times as you can bear. Any copywriting guru worth their salt, if they're being honest, will tell you to do this. You could be told all the greatest copywriting secrets in the world, but if you haven't got this basic foundation to build on, they'll be useless.

If you want to truly understand the art of getting people to click and harness the power of direct-response copywriting, take some time today to look for successful long copy sales letters. Study them. Look to see what's working well and copy it out by hand as many times as you can.

Make the effort to do that and you'll already be a hundred steps ahead of any other wannabe copywriter.

And believe me, by putting this work in now – remember, it's only really an hour here and there – in the weeks and months to come you will soon see it pay off as you'll soon be writing better copy than you ever knew you could.

Keep up the habit

Please take note, just because you've copied out one or two sales letters, don't think you should never do so again. You simply cannot stop learning when it comes to direct-response copywriting. There will always be new developments, new techniques and new challenges in the field and it is only by reading new sales letters – at least one a day, ideally – that you'll be able to advance to and stay on top of your game.

Even if what you choose to read on a given day is a pile of pants, you should still read it. Analyse why it is so bad, take it apart and then make sure that your own writing does not make the mistakes you've just identified. The fact is: you can always take something useful from a piece of someone else's promotional writing, be that promotion good, bad or downright ugly.

Venture forth and make a promise to yourself to read at least one new sales promotion every day from now on. And every now and then, copy one out by hand. It'll help, I promise.

Top Tip

When it comes to finding successful long copy sales letters, a good resource is affiliate networks like Clickbank and JVZoo. They basically act as a marketplace for people to sell their products and services and obviously, in doing so, there are hundreds of long copy sales letters posted there. Not all of them will be good, but you can see from the sales figures which ones are worth looking at and potentially copying out. Visit: **www.clickbank.com** and **www.JVZoo.com**.

Chapter Three
Understanding Your Audience

"When I'm making a film, I'm the audience."

— **Martin Scorsese**

The myth of knowing your audience

"Know your audience," they say. As far as a piece of advice goes, *know your audience* is as useless as it is meaningless. And really, it's a massive misconception. Think about it. When most people say *know your audience*, what do they mean? Take my friend T's somewhat blue best man speech at a wedding I went to many years ago. In my opinion — as a member of the wedding's audience — best man speeches are supposed to be a bit blue. Yes, they need to congratulate the bride and groom, but I think they're meant to be a bit risky too. It's traditional to reveal the odd rude story from the groom's past. I thought T's speech was funny, as did many others there. Some less so. How come?

Trouble is, at a wedding you get all sorts of people: old and young, the thick-skinned, the easily offended, the humorous and the humourless. And it's not just weddings — this is universal. It's the same for any occasion where you are required to communicate to more than one person. Let's say you're at a gardening event doing a talk about irrigation. Know your audience, they say. OK then, your audience is 200 gardeners. Sorted. You know that all gardeners are exactly the same, right? If you're into gardening, you must be a certain age, have specific extra-gardening interests, enjoy specific days out, and find only certain types of jokes amusing. In other words, all 200 people, because they are into gardening, must be exactly the same. Of course not. Everyone is different.

What about this book? You're reading this now. So that must mean you're exactly the same as Keith who's reading this on his lunch hour in a quiet office in Basingstoke, right? You both like the same television programmes, the same comedians, the same music. Don't you? Do you heck!

You're an individual. You have your own interests, your own nuances that define who you are. Old Keith, out there in his quiet Basingstoke office, he has his own interests and nuances too. But what if you and Keith were both gardeners? What if you had to sit through a dull speech about irrigation? You'd want it to be jazzed up a bit, right? Problem is: Keith doesn't. He likes his irrigation talks boring and bland. You can see the problem.

The fact is, to successfully communicate to large, varied audiences, whether speaking or writing, it's no good (and impossible) to know your audience as a single entity. If you try to cater for everyone, your communication will be dull, and any idea you're trying to communicate will likely be forgotten pretty darn quick. But there are some things you can do to help…

Four tips for speaking to your audience

1. Speak to a single person

Don't try to talk to your entire audience in one go. Always speak to a single person. Some people will tell you to come up with a back story of a specific person; who they are, what they do, what they want from life, and so on. Here's a better way round that. Why invent someone? There's no need. Picture the person you're talking to as one of your actual friends. Sometimes your real friends disagree with you too. But do you change the way you speak to them? No. Because communicating with a friend is always genuine. Speaking to a large audience should be the same. And being genuine, you should remember…

2. The idea above all else

The idea you're communicating is always the most important aspect. Some people might disagree with your idea, others might whole heartedly agree, but you should never let the possible perception of the idea sway your communication of it. You must be honest to the idea. If you believe in what you're saying, you'll be able to reasonably argue with anyone who disagrees with it. At the same time...

3. Avoid causing needless offence

You shouldn't be bland, but neither should you use language or stories that are needlessly offensive. Swearing, for example, is known to upset a lot of people whilst doing little to enhance an argument or idea (remember, the idea above all else). Though you might swear a lot normally, when communicating to a large audience, is it worth the risk? You'll soon see it's not. And finally...

4. Be yourself

People try to complicate things. They think that if you are talking or writing to a load of people you need to affect some kind of professional delivery. Come off it. If you were telling your partner you love them would you adopt an increased professionalism? "May I be so bold as to declare my affections for you?" or "Your appearance today is of an excellent standard." I don't think so. Does talking like that make your idea any more effective? No. In fact, it makes it less effective. "I love you," and "You look gorgeous," are both much more natural and will be more effective.

Remember to always talk or write how you normally would in a normal situation and you'll find that you're able to communicate your ideas a lot more genuinely and effectively.

Keep the customers coming back

I'm the kind of guy whom you're likely to bump into at a run-down pub checking out a £5-entry post-rock gig. But here I was, herded into Sheffield Arena about to watch Drake – perhaps the third most successful rapper working today, after Kendrick Lamar and Kanye.

You see, I've inadvertently built up quite an in-depth knowledge of modern hip-hop. I've seen Kendrick Lamar, Mac Miller, A$AP Rocky, 2 Chains… the list goes on. Some I actually enjoy, others not so much.

But anyway, here I am – amongst the scantily clad youth of Sheffield and the surrounding area – to see the third top dog in this game: Canadian rapper, Drake. Little do I realise I'm about to witness a master class in engaging your audience. The show was fair enough. Drake ran through most of his hits. And the performance itself was full of energy. But what really impressed me was this guy's awareness of his audience.

Come again?

In business, the real secret to long-term success is to keep your customers coming back. In fact, getting one customer to pay twice is often easier than finding a brand new customer. This means that renewal copy – the copy that encourages a customer's repeat business – is incredibly important. And that's why Drake was so impressive. He did three things, which I think you can learn a lot from.

First, for large sections of the show, images of the audience were projected onto the huge screens behind the stage. Not only was the quality of these images unnervingly good – affording you the odd feeling you were watching the live DVD at the same time as the actual live performance – it also gave the crowd the sensation of being truly involved in the show. I expect every fan who saw their face on the screen behind Drake would rush to buy the DVD on its release, just to see if they can spot themselves again.

The next clever thing he did was invite on stage a rather sturdy woman from the crowd and serenade her. Now, this isn't a new conceit. Artists have been bringing audience members on stage and singing at them for decades.

But here Drake was particularly clever by not bringing on the type of woman you'd typically expect him to. If you've ever seen a modern pop video on MTV, you'll know they tend to feature unrealistically thin women. Instead, Drake serenaded a larger woman and did so genuinely, with no obvious cynicism. A cynical choice or not, by doing so he endeared himself to women of all shapes and sizes, giving everyone an equal chance to dream that next time, it could be them. All good so far, but the finale was his masterpiece.

Having spent the vast majority of the show on stage, he spent the final hour walking around above the crowd on a hydraulic runway that was lowered from the arena ceiling. Getting into the crowd like this was visually good, but the best thing was what he did once he was in the crowd. You see, for what must have been a good 30–45 minutes, he bounded around this runway and performed an off-the-cuff rap about all the people (mostly women) he could see in the audience.

He pointed out that girl with the blonde hair and told her how pretty she was. He pointed out that girl with the pink t-shirt and told her how sexy she was. He pointed out that bloke with the Drake t-shirt on and thanked him for his support. Now, I hope he was making up as he went along, but something tells me everything he said was pretty damn generic and could be repeated to equal effect on any given night. (Maybe I'm just sore he didn't seem to spot me, despite being the only guy wearing a tweed jacket and scarf. Perhaps I just wasn't projecting myself properly.)

The point is, by going around and pointing people out like this, Drake was cleverly drumming up repeat business in a very direct way: all the women (and men, for that matter) who thought Drake called them out will no doubt be quick to buy his next record. They have a connection now.

It works. At the time of writing, Drake's second record had sold around 2.2 million copies in the US. It'd been out two years and four months.

His third record had already sold 1.5 million in the US and it had been out just six months.

It's interesting, right? And when we come back to copywriting, I think there's a good lesson here: that at all times you should be looking to involve your audience. You need to make them a part of the story you're telling. If you can do this from the initial sales message, you're on to a winner.

You should use this same technique in your sales writing. How? Well, as I've said before, you should assess your audience and understand what common ideas they think about, what common beliefs they hold, what common things they do. Sure, as we saw earlier, it's impossible to 'know your audience' on a mass scale. But if you can reference these specific things and give the illusion you're speaking directly to individuals about the thoughts they have, that's good. It's all about the research. In fact, if you're having trouble connecting with your audience, I almost guarantee it has nothing to do with your writing, but more to do with the fact that you haven't properly researched the person you specifically want to speak to.

I'm not recommending you go out and listen to Drake. But I do recommend you learn from his ability to connect with his customers in a very convincing way to ensure that they keep coming back to buy album after album and ticket after ticket.

The punch line? A few weeks after seeing Drake, I went for a meal with my brother and his girlfriend in London. I mentioned that I'd been to see Drake. My brother's girlfriend, being a huge Drake fan, explained that she'd been too. But she'd been to the Manchester show. How was it, I asked? "Oh, Glenn, it was amazing," she told me excitedly. "He came into the crowd and he was pointing people out and he came round to where we were stood and I was wearing this yellow dress and waving and he waved back and shouted out to ME!"

The challenge of persuasion

I'm writing this section following a field trip to Delray Beach, Florida. I was there for a copywriting conference held by the American Writers and Artists Institute (AWAI). As it's the home of many successful information publishers, I've been visiting Delray for many years to regularly catch up with some of the top writers in the direct-response copywriting industry. But that's not why I suggest you take a field trip of your own today. Instead, it comes off the back of a discussion I once had about what *understanding direct-response copywriting* actually means. You see, the chap I was speaking to suggested that direct-response copywriting is about understanding how to write a long copy sales letter. And he believes that's essentially it. I disagree. Strongly.

Of course, as a direct-response copywriter it goes without saying that the ability to write a long copy sales letter is incredibly useful and it's for that reason we're focusing on them in this book. As I said before, everything in direct-response copy flows from understanding how to write a long copy sales letter. And after all, direct-response copy has a very close relationship with long copy. Historically, the two phrases have gone hand-in-hand.

I guess the reason is that you stand more chance of getting a direct-response from a reader if you take your time to persuade them with a long copy argument. The problem is, this natural association of direct-response and long copy misleads people to the same conclusion this chap has come to. The truth is, the technical side of specifically *writing* a sales letter only covers part of the direct-response story.

When it comes to understanding direct-response copy, it is even more important that you take the time to learn about the emotional side of things. You see, to become a true direct-response copywriting master, you need to know what makes people tick. Or, in other words, you need to delve into the psychology behind what influences people. And not just in regard to buying decisions!

Remember, as a copywriter you're passing messages on to real people. You need to explore what makes people make any decision — be it which socks to wear on a certain day, or which route they take to work. You must spend a hell of a lot of time studying your readers – or as they're more commonly called: humans. That's why I suggest you take a field trip. I'll tell you where in the next chapter.

For now, the key thing is that you understand direct-response copywriting is not just about the **act** of writing long copy sales letters to get people to buy stuff. It's about **presenting** an idea to a **person** and **persuading** them to take **a direct action** at the end. That is where the direct-response element comes from. It's got nothing to do with the length of the copy or the format of a sales letter.

A sales letter is just that: a format. Much like a PPC ad is another format. Or a squeeze page. Or a coupon you clip off the corner of a page in a magazine. Indeed, many of the technical issues I discuss later in this book (e.g. concise language, clear sentence structure) could easily be applied to different formats of direct-response copywriting.

On the point of worrying less about the format and more about the reader, advertising expert Dave Trott said much the same thing when I saw him speak at the Professional Copywriters' Network conference in London a few years back. He was speaking about the various social media platforms, but his sentiment was the same. Facebook, Twitter, Snapchat: they're all just formats for delivering a message to a reader. Though the format may change, the reader remains the same. For this reason, Trott agrees you should focus your studies on the reader. Not the format.

Founder of the information-publishing giant, The Agora, Bill Bonner, similarly argued for more reader-focused copy in his keynote speech at an American Writers and Artists Institute conference. He suggested that good copy should make the reader the hero. I agree.

Top Tip

Write with a specific reader in mind. The more detail you can build up around this reader the better. I would recommend choosing a family member. Who you settle on may depend on the product or service you're writing copy for. If the product is targeted at an older generation, write your copy as though you're speaking directly to your granddad. If a teenager will ultimately read the copy, you should look to a younger sibling or niece/nephew. In targeting your copy at a specific person you already know, it will make the copy more authentic and more relatable for a wider audience.

Chapter Four
Doing Your Research

> *"Inspiration is hard to come by. You have to take it where you find it."*
>
> — **Bob Dylan**

Are you writing true enough?

These days it's almost cliché to say so. But I find the writing of Ernest Hemingway such a useful resource as a copywriter. If you're not regularly reading his work, you should be. You'll learn far more about good copy reading *The Old Man and the Sea* than boring yourself with most of the junk copywriting books out there.

More often that not, when it comes to taking advice from Hemingway's writing, people focus on the simplicity of the syntax. Advice is taken on a technical level: keep your language plain, your sentences short.

But sitting here reading in a small café in Cleethorpes (Riverhead Coffee on St Peter's Avenue – a good cup of coffee for those interested in such things), I came across a passage that touches on something I often try to teach to new copywriters. It's something less technical. Less tangible, even. Have a read yourself:

> "If a writer of prose knows enough of what he is writing about he may omit things that he knows and the reader, if the writer is writing truly enough, will have a feeling of those things as strongly as though the writer had stated them. The dignity of movement of an iceberg is due to only one-eighth of it being

above water. A writer who omits things because he does not know them only makes hollow places in his writing."

It's taken from his novel about bullfighting, *Death in the Afternoon* – an excellent book, which I'd highly recommend. And his sentiment is an important one. You see, as a copywriter, if you've done enough research and truly understand the product or service and write about it in an authentic way, the reader will naturally sense your belief in the product or service.

How? I can't honestly say; I prefer to call it the magic of good copy. Wishy-washy, I know. But seriously. It's not something you can – or should – attempt to tie down. It's a gut feeling thing. Some people just get it. For others, it takes a little longer to click. You know when someone seems to be leading you down a garden path and something in their tone, or in the words they're using, or something in their eyes, their smile, gives it away? Whatever it is, it doesn't quite sit right? It's like that, but in writing. As I say, it's really a question of authenticity, just as Hemingway is suggesting in that extract.

Don't get me wrong, the very best copywriters in the world are pretty good at faking authenticity and will have done so at some point in their career. But I dare say if you asked a copywriter to explain how they made their most successful promotion sound so authentic, it'll be because they truly believed it themselves.

That's the rub, you see. There is no big secret behind writing successful copy and getting that all important click. As Hemingway says: you just need to write truly enough. Of course, on the flipside, if you're lazy and are tempted to skirt over details that you haven't bothered to investigate, it will be equally clear to the reader. They'll spot the "hollow places" in your copy. You could refer to those hollow places as unanswered objections.

Don't skimp on your research. Without doubt the easiest route to successful copy is to dig deep into the product or service itself. To borrow from Hemingway's metaphor, find the bottom of the iceberg. Understand it and admire it and then, when it comes to sharing your findings with others, you'll know enough and, if you write truly enough, your reader will have a feel as strongly towards the product or service as you do. Or in other words, they'll want to buy.

You won't learn much without leaving the house

Right now, I want you to take a field trip. The trip isn't to any particular place, but wherever you might choose to take your field trip, the only stipulation is that it is a place inhabited by lots of other people. I recommend a local café. Or the supermarket. Or one of those slightly larger, open-plan high street banks. The key thing is that you're able to observe people. Indeed, that's all I want you to do. For five minutes, half an hour, or as long as you're able, just watch people and see how they act when faced with a choice.

If you choose the café – look at how people analyse the menu. Or do they already know what they want without consultation? Or do they ask questions of the person serving? Perhaps they look to the person ahead in the queue to lead them? Just watch and think about it. In a situation like this, where people are actively making a choice, you can pick up on similarities between people, and target them in copy. It could be something as simple as noticing that when people are given a menu, they often ignore the food and go straight to the drinks. You could use this common trait to relate to readers in your copy.

Same rules apply in the supermarket – why does one shopper choose brand X? Do they pause? Do they peruse? Do they pick up two different brands of cereal and compare nutritional facts? Just watch and think about it. It might be interesting to note that people will often consider the luxury brand of a certain product first, turning it over in their hands, before opting for the cheaper supermarket own brand option. Such a process speaks of the aspirational nature of your possible customers. They wish they could afford the more expensive option. You can speak to that emotion in your copy.

In the bank you can just as easily see choices being made. Watch people decide how much to pay into their savings. See how they delay over how much cash to withdraw. Notice how they choose which paying-in slip they need. Just watch and think about it. The end game for most pieces of copy is to get the customer to spend money in someway. That's why it's interesting to see how people are with money. If they're protective of their card details in a bank, they're sure going to be protective when it comes to buying something online. Understanding this means you can begin to address those concerns with your writing.

Of course, during your field trip, try not to look too strange. But, if all else fails, just start tapping your phone as though you've received an interesting text. Few people take notice of others texting. Regardless of how you may look to others, I do hope you take my suggestion of a field trip on board. Hanging around a supermarket may sound silly, but dedicating time to observe your customer is incredibly important. It will provide you with a solid base upon which you can build your more focused research into the emotions that influence people's decision-making.

Remember, it's your ability to understand your reader that will allow you to write more effective copy, regardless of whether that copy is direct or indirect, long or short, online or off. The format doesn't matter; only your reader does.

A universal truth

You're in Normandy, France. You're far from any real form of civilization, just a few old brick buildings set back from winding roads and rolling hay fields. One of these old buildings is a large 16th century chateau, owned by Bill Bonner, founder of information publishing giant, The Agora. In the building are gathered copywriters from all around the world, with one aim: to discuss copywriting and compare notes. You look at headlines that work and those that don't. You look at persuasion techniques that can have a huge effect on the customer's ordering process. You look at how pricing can completely change the way you approach a piece of copy. You meet copywriters from India, Brazil, Argentina, Spain, Australia and even China, and it's interesting to see some of the different copywriting challenges people face in their particular markets. But even more interesting is how **not** different things are when you really scratch below the surface.

What are you really writing about?

This was me, a few years back, when I was starting out in the world of direct-response copywriting. And as I listened to the different copywriters explain their projects to me, I realised one of the biggest errors most copywriters make – and this especially applies to newer writers – is that they simply don't know enough about the product they're selling.

When you can write authentically about something – be it a product you've used, a song you've listened to, an emotion you've felt – a magical thing happens that simply cannot be trained. When you write truthfully, readers notice that.

The problem with many copywriters – new and old – is they write what they think they're supposed to write. They've read so much old copy and learnt to mimic the content and delivery so well that what they produce looks and reads exactly as it should. But the magic is missing. It's not real. It's literally *copy*.

Don't write until you're ready

I've experienced the problem myself. When I thought about doing an MA in creative writing, I wrote a short detective story and gave it to my tutor to read. It's very good, he said, but it's just like Paul Auster. At the time, I was appalled. What do you mean *but*? That's a good thing isn't it? I loved Paul Auster (and still do), so to have written an Auster-esque story was surely an achievement. Of course, it wasn't. I'd merely emulated something good. The fake was a good one, but a fake all the same. The story needed to be rewritten in my own voice. It needed to be authentic. And so, at the time, I decided I wasn't ready for an MA. I needed to do more research. I needed to find out more about myself, about my voice. I needed to dig deeper to find my authenticity. I recommend you do the same with your copy.

Don't start writing just yet. You see, no matter how qualified you might be, I'm sure there's more research you could do. Something more you could find out about the product you're writing for, so when you share your insight with the reader it blows them away. To do this, you must keep asking *why*. Keep digging into the story, into the product itself. Read as much as you can with the *why* at the front of your mind. Ask customers who've tried the product why they like it. Quiz the product creator on why they created the product in the first place.

For example, if the creator of a health product thinks you shouldn't use prescription drugs, ask him why. And when he tells you it's because of a book he read on the subject, ask him why he read that book in the first place. And when he tells you that a local shaman who practices medicine in a small wooden hut in Uganda gave it to him, you've got a much more authentic story already.

Or if the editor of a financial newsletter says you should invest in gold, ask him why. And when he tells you it's because gold has been going down and he thinks it's going to turn around, ask him why. When he tells you that he's just spent the last two weeks deconstructing the Bank of England's monetary policy with a crack team of Oxbridge economists, you're on your way to a more authentic story.

My point is that you must dig deeper. It's not enough to just know the rough idea behind a product, how much it costs, what the customer gets and then just fit it into an old piece of copy.

You need to know more about what you're selling than the person selling it. I realise that might be impossible, but aim high! Sure, it's more work in the short term. But it'll repay you in the end.

Top Tip

When it comes to researching for a copy project, you should always split your research into two tiers. Think of the first tier as the fundamental research itself. This is all the initial reading of books and searching of the web. Let's say you're writing a blog post for a sofa company. The sofa company have recently started supplying sofas to a national coffee chain and they want to shout about it to potential new coffee shops looking for new sofas. Not being an expert on sofas, you search online for something interesting about the industry and you find out how these sofas are made is actually quite interesting. At this stage of first-tier research, because you're not an expert and because you've probably only looked for stuff online, everything is potentially interesting to you. But the fact is, almost everyone in the sofa industry and those coffee shops looking to buy new sofas already know about how the sofas are made. It's not news to the customer... it's only news to you, the copywriter.

That's why, once you've done your first tier of research, you've got to go again. You've got to go deeper. You've got to look into the points of interest you discovered and figure out which of them are already known in the industry and which are genuinely new discoveries. The key here is to understand the value of that first-tier research in bringing you up to speed in the industry you're writing for... and then pushing yourself on and adding a second tier of research that really digs much deeper.

Chapter Five
The Importance of Good Ideas

"I begin with an idea and then it becomes something else."

— *Pablo Picasso*

Starting in the mind

Before you can start writing your copy, you need an angle to approach from. But how do you find it? Most marketing people will tell you that the key to any successful business is testing. But there's a little more to it. And to explain, I'm going to enlist the help of a theoretical physicist! Huh?!

Believe it or not, successful marketing shares much with a fundamental principle of science. You see, in his 'Lectures on Physics', theoretical physicist Richard P. Feynman says: "The test of all knowledge is experiment." Reading his lectures, that quote stuck out. But even more interesting is what Feynman goes on to ask: "…what is the source of knowledge?" And "where do the laws that are to be tested come from?" Now, on first look that's all a bit profound for this book on direct-response copywriting. But the answers lie in a simple three-stage cycle that you can use to increase the effectiveness of marketing for any type of business.

The test of all knowledge is experiment

Say you've produced a new book on weight loss for men. OK, good stuff. Now you need to tell people about it and sell some copies. You write the advertising copy. Question is, how do you pitch it, and who do you pitch it to? Naturally, your first idea would probably be to pitch it at men. Do you want to lose weight? Yes? Then you want this book!

But hang on, because you could scare men into buying it – if you don't read this book, you'll get fatter. Or you could use hope – if you read this book, you'll get thinner. Which is the better angle? Here we're back to Feynman's original line: "The test of all knowledge is experiment." So, you experiment. You try both angles and see which one works best.

Experimenting, however, only helps us to come to a conclusion in the sense that it gives us hints. Let's say the fear angle comes out top in the experiment. Men are fearful of not losing weight. This is a hint at something bigger.

The three-stage cycle of successful marketing

Feynman goes on to say that what is also needed is:

> "…imagination to create from these hints the great generalizations – to guess at the wonderful, simple, but very strange patterns beneath… and then to experiment to check again whether we have made the right guess."

We have the hint. Men are fearful of putting on weight. Now we must use our imagination. We must go deeper – why are men fearful of putting on weight? Could it be because they will think themselves less attractive? Could be. And it follows then that men want to attract women… so a good guess would be that a better way to sell your book on weight loss would be to aim it at helping men to attract women. And another guess… men are fearful that women will not like them if they are overweight. It's fair to assume this is not unfounded. So we can guess that women are interested in the weight of men. Could there then be women out there who want their men to lose weight? Could we aim the book at those women? "Is your man a little loose round the waist? Of course he is, but this book will make him thin!" To check these we experiment again, we test our guesses.

For the sake of argument, let's imagine the result is that we actually find books on men's weight loss sell best to women. This is a brand new generalisation – one that, in this example, increases your profitability. Without experiment, imagination and testing, we might never have discovered this. We can look at those three factors as a repeating cycle. An initial experiment provides fuel for the imagining process, which provides ideas for testing, the results of which may give new reasons for experimentation.

Whatever field of business you may be involved with, to discover the great generalisations, the marketing laws that work best, those that lead to the greatest profit, you should follow this simple three-stage process.

1. Make your initial *experiment*. Try it, see what happens.

2. Go through the *imagining* process. What bigger ideas does your initial experiment hint at? Develop them and have a guess at what the bigger ideas could be.

3. *Test* those ideas. Check to see if your guess were right.

You'll be amazed at the new marketing ideas you discover.

Rereading Ogilvy

While writing this book, I reread David Ogilvy's *Ogilvy on Advertising*. It's an incredibly useful resource. There are so many ideas that Ogilvy discusses that I'd be here all day if I tried to tell you about all of them. For now, in these pages of my own book, I just want to share one overall idea Ogilvy's kept going back to. It's dead simple and total common sense. The tricky part is always being able to remember to stick to it yourself. It's hard; I often stray and end up falling foul of this basic principle. When it comes to communicating ideas: **don't try to be too clever.**

Whatever idea you're communicating – advice, news, a product or service, a thought – that idea must take priority in the message. Being a creative sort myself, this is an extremely difficult pill to swallow. Natural instinct encourages you to be as original as possible, whenever possible. This presents a big problem in business. Of course, originality always has a place and new methods will always find a way through if they are truly effective. But too often this desire for originality means ideas that have already been proven to work are forgotten.

I have often made the mistake of obscuring an idea by trying to represent it in an original way. I was trying to be too clever and therefore failed to communicate the idea. If I had looked at what had worked before, kept it simple and presented the **idea** as priority and not the **presentation** of the idea, I would have had much greater success. To make sure you communicate the ideas of your business effectively, always remember to keep it simple, refer to what has already been proven to work, and above all do not try to be too clever.

You can try to be original, but you'll make less money

Here's the problem, though. People love being original. They love coming up with new ways to get an idea across.

I saw an advert in the cinema for Absolute Vodka years ago that stuck in my mind. Did you ever see this? It goes along with people hugging and kissing and shaking hands instead of paying for things. And then declares that "It's an absolute world," and that we should buy Absolute Vodka.

Now, maybe I'm missing something, but the series of images that precede this message don't relate to the message (buy vodka) at all, and frankly put me off the message, essentially leaving me confused. If I am missing the message, that means other people like me could be too, and that means there's a percentage of the audience not getting the message.

According to Absolut themselves, the advert "depicts scenes from a more vibrant world as envisioned by the brand, the 'Hugs' [advert] sends a spirit of community, suggesting that 'In an ABSOLUT World', money can be replaced by acts of kindness." Good, good. And pray tell, what does that have to do with vodka? Show me someone who thinks boozing on vodka instils a sense of anything other than drunkenness. The message has been lost. All because the advert's director, whose previous work includes Britney Spears and Kanye West videos, together with the creative guys behind the scenes, thought they'd be original.

The important thing to remember is to make the idea the priority and not the presentation. Always do that and you'll always be able to communicate your advice, news, product, service or thought effectively.

The CIA secret for identifying good ideas

Before you write any piece of copy, you need to figure out if your idea is any good. If your idea sucks ass, your copy will suck ass. Worse: a bad idea will make it even harder to write the suck-ass copy.

On the flipside: if your idea is good, writing the copy will be much easier, and faster. And chances are, your copy will be much more effective. So, before you write a word, you need to be able to identify if your idea is any good. Luckily, I've come up with a simple, three-step formula to help you identify good ideas. Oh, and by chance it also happens to spell CIA: Confirm, Inform and Astound.

Confirm

Your idea must be inherently sound, believable and prove something the reader suspected was true. All good ideas are grounded in smart thinking and make sense. That might sound obvious, but you'd be surprised by how much copy gets put in front of me that is a result of bad thinking and which makes no sense.

For an example of it being done well, take a piece of copy written by a top, top US copywriter and a very nice guy called Scott Bardelli. He wrote a breakthrough piece of copy that has become known as 'The Pot Promo'. The basic premise of the copy was that in the run up to the vote on legalising cannabis in the US, it would make good sense to invest in various marijuana companies that could see big gains if legalisation went through. Inherently the idea makes sense. Pot made legal. More people want pot. Pot companies do better business. Hurrah. The proof is in the pudding: the copy Scott wrote worked very well. Reasonableness is something to remember when it comes to identifying good ideas.

Another example from the advertising history books is the famous Volkswagen "Think Small" campaign of the 1960s. The series of adverts featured small images of the Volkswagen Beetle and the simple headline "Think Small." Here the writers had the intention to confirm what people thought about American cars being big and European cars being small. Rather than try to persuade the reader to change their mind about such preconceptions, they confirmed it and made it a selling point. Very simple. But very effective.

Too many people think good ideas need to be big ideas. They think they have to be incredible. But by aiming too high, they make their ideas literally incredible, i.e. **not** credible. Don't be fooled into thinking your idea is good because it's wild.

And don't try to change people's minds. People buy good ideas they want to believe. You can't (or at least it's stupidly hard and a waste of time to try to) sell someone on something they don't already believe. As an example, consider the most successful piece of long copy in the past ten years: 'The End of America'. This copy has been adapted all around the world and has helped make millions. Why? There are many reasons. But fundamentally, it spoke about something people already believed: that most developed countries in the modern world have a huge problem with debt. People already suspected that was the case… it wasn't a wild idea… and it made sense. Simple.

So, that's step one: make sure your idea is inherently sound, believable and that it proves something the reader already suspects is true.

Inform

Step two? Your idea must teach the reader something new that only a true expert on the subject would know. Mike Palmer is one of the best direct-response copywriters in the world. But you probably haven't heard of him – he keeps himself behind the scenes.

I've been lucky enough to see him speak a couple of times. One of the things I always remember about a speech he gave was the thought that when it comes to identifying good ideas, you need to make sure that the idea teaches the reader something few other people know. You can't be sold on your own naivety to an idea.

As copywriters we have the impossible task of becoming an expert on the subject we're writing about... and then we have to find out what the experts don't even know. It's tough – but essential. If you run with an idea that is already widely understood by those in the industry and you try to present it as something wildly new, it's going to make you look foolish.

Looking at it slightly differently, you need to define what makes your idea unique. And I mean the idea, not the copy. Before you even try to make your copy unique, you need to make your idea unique.

So, what have we got so far? An inherently sound idea that confirms what people already think, but informs them of a unique new element that they've not come across. Cool, now we just need to take one more step.

Astound

Your idea must be delivered in a new and simple way that shocks and intrigues the reader. This is where we start to introduce the principles of good copywriting. If you've properly considered your idea in light of the first two steps, writing the copy itself is going to be much easier. As I said at the start, writing copy for genuinely new and unique ideas will always be faster and, most likely, more effective.

At this final stage, you need to figure out how you can astound people with your idea. For me, this goes back to Eugene Schwartz's idea of customer awareness. You need to establish what level of awareness your audience has about your idea. For example, let's say you were selling washing machines in 1908 (which is when they were invented, interestingly... in Chicago). At that stage you could go to market and say: "Imagine if you could put all your dirty clothes in a box and then take them out an hour later and they'd be clean." People would think you were some kind of wonderful washing witch. But fast forward to today and people would laugh you out of the room for advertising washing machines in this way, hence adverts for washing machines these days involving weird futuristic science.

In 1908, awareness of washing machines was very low, so just the basic idea was astounding. By 2018, I expect only an advert that promises the washing machine will also make beer from the dirt of your clothes will be effective.

How do you test customer awareness of your idea? One thing to definitely not do is only share it with other copywriters, or marketers, or people inside your business. They will have too much baggage, they will want to prove they already understand the idea, and they'll be biased depending on whether they like you or not. Instead you should take your idea on the road and test it with as many random people as you can, who have no stake in your business at all. I'm talking about your partner, your mother, your friend next door, even the guy in the corner shop who is weirdly over familiar every time you go in… ask what he thinks. Bottom line is: don't wait to test an idea out after you've written your copy – that's dumb.

Use the steps I've outlined above to identify whether you've got a good idea on your hands. If you have, go for it. If you haven't, save yourself a headache and rethink it.

Ideas are irritating

Sometimes ideas are right there in your face, shouting at you like an arrogant teenage kid who thinks they know best. Other times they're nowhere to be seen, like your broke mate Steve who's always in the toilet when it's his round at the bar. I'll tell you what. From now on, let's boycott ideas. Who needs them anyway? Not me.

Well. Er. Hmmm. That's the problem. I do need them. And so do you. If you want to learn how to get people to click on your copy, the one thing you'll need in abundance – more than any other skill, in fact – is the ability to come up with good ideas. They are at the root of all good copy. I'm sure you don't need me to tell you: without a strong idea backing it up, any piece of copy will be limp, full of waffle and ultimately a failure (or a *bomb*, as it's known in the trade). Whether it's a 50-page direct-response sales letter or a three-line PPC advert, it needs an idea behind it or it's going to suck. I think most proven copywriters will admit, the ability to come up with good ideas can cover almost any other flaw you might have as a writer. Can't spell so good? Don't worry, that's what spellcheck is for. Not too hot on grammar? Who cares, read your copy aloud or get someone to read over it for you. Struggle to edit yourself? Waffling isn't ideal, but a thumb over each sentence will show you which ones aren't necessary and they're easily deleted.

But here's the catch…

If you can't think up new ideas, you've got a major problem and you need to fix it ASAP. How? Quite simply it's a matter of balance: if you want something new to come out of your brain, you've got to put something new in. You see, your brain is like Audrey II from *The Little Shop of Horrors*: it demands to be fed. Ideas are like those new shops you suddenly notice have opened. You can't remember seeing the premises being renovated or new signs being put up – just one day it wasn't there and today it is. But just because you didn't notice the work being done doesn't mean it wasn't. Ideas are definitely built.

Only problem is, ideas are built in your subconscious (which is why you don't see them being built) and it's difficult – no scratch that – it's impossible to know exactly which raw materials you need to build them. Therefore you need as many different raw materials as you can get your hands on. The good news is: anything is useful, from high-brow literature to crappy reality television. In fact, the one thing I would recommend when it comes to feeding your brain with the raw material you need to subconsciously build ideas is this:

> Consume equal amounts of content that is related to copywriting and content that is unrelated to copywriting.

The importance of raw material

Therefore, sure, read Cialdini's *Influence* and by all means read whatever colourfully designed paperback the Heath brothers have on the market at the moment. (Chip and Dan Heath are the authors of *The Power of Moments*, *Switch* and *Made to Stick*, among others – all recommended.) And yes, as any good copywriter worth their salt will advise, you should read one piece of copy a day (or at least one a week) to stay on top of your game. But don't stop there. To give you an idea of how much random stuff you need to consume to come up with new ideas, here's what raw material I credit with helping write two recent pieces of long copy:

- Three graphic novels: one a biography of Fidel Castro, one an account of Freud's most famous patient (The Wolfman) and one about the famous flapper girl Kiki of Montparnasse.

- Three fiction books: *The Brief and Wondrous Life of Oscar Wao* by Junot Diaz, *Death in the Andes* by Mario Vargas Llosa, and *Motherless Brooklyn* by Jonathan Lethem.

- Two non-fiction books: *How Music Works* by David Byrne and *Predictably Irrational* by Dan Ariely (strictly I was re-reading this).

- In honesty I've read about five sales promotions in full: one oldie by Bill Bonner and another by Mark Ford, one of my own and two newer ones by friends, one that flew and one that bombed. Oh, and the packs other writers have asked me to review.

- I've watched four films: *The Secret Life of Pets* and *Despicable Me 3*, which are both obviously children's films; *Scenes from a Mall*, which was a favour Woody Allen must have owed someone; and *The Squid and the Whale*, about a literary couple going through a divorce.

- I've also been intermittently re-watching *The Sopranos*, strangely watching a reality television show in the UK called *The Voice*, which aims to find the best singer in the country (and is actually quite addictive), and I've been to see a couple of games of football, in varying divisions.

- And finally I've been listening to new records by Iron & Wine, Mogwai and the Effects.

Sounds tiring, right? Especially when you consider that during my consumption of all this random raw material I also spent a week in Amsterdam, where I visited the Rijksmuseum and the slightly less salubrious Hemp museum. All in all that's just over a month's worth of input into my brain and obviously that's not counting the stuff that I picked up from interacting with people on a day-to-day basis, talking in the pub over a few pints, and catching up on phone and email.

I don't list all this stuff to try to impress you with my cultural consumption. Instead, I want to illustrate my point: it's a lot of random raw material. Just think what all that is doing in my mind.

Take a detail I read about how Fidel Castro could have been killed before any of his revolutionary business if it wasn't for one sympathetic soldier sending him to a public prison. Think how that might interact with watching a surprisingly emotional performance by a singer on *The Voice*. How – or even if – this information will appear directly in my future copy, we simply do not know. The detail about Castro could influence a passage about chance, perhaps, and how small decisions have huge consequences. The singer might inspire a passage about ignoring what others think and following your dreams. Who knows? What we do know is that my brain now has a vast resource of raw material to delve into and potentially build from.

Once you've fed your brain, to write good copy, you must trust it to do its work. Yes there are exercises you can do to tease out ideas and by consciously separating the left and right sides of your brain you can encourage new thoughts. But ultimately, the ability to come up with new ideas is fundamental to your success as a persuader. And in turn, the one thing that any copywriter of any level must do to develop and maintain that ability, is to always keep feeding your brain with a vast variety of raw materials.

The power of one

Stick to one idea.

The more I think about it, it's probably the simplest but most effective piece of advice I've ever received. Mark Ford – one of the master copywriters who taught me it – calls it the *power of one*. Writes Mark:

> "It struck me that readers didn't want to hear everything I had to say about a topic every time I wrote. They were looking for a single, useful suggestion or idea that could make them more successful."

It's been called many things, but the principle remains the same. When it comes to any form of writing, but especially writing to sell, it is so important (I'm talking make or break here) that you stick to one message.

Your partner asks you to do three things – the dishes, the rubbish, the ironing. No chance you're doing all three. At best, you'll do two, badly. You receive an e-letter. It invites you to read three different messages. Not likely. At best, you'll read one, skim the rest. You see a menu on the side of an ice cream van. It offers you 20 options. Were you planning on buying 20 ice creams? Of course not. That would be one heck of a brain freeze!

Apply the power of one to those messages.

Darling, can you clean the dishes? Of course you can and you will. The ice cream seller has one large sign that says '99s with a flake'. What are you having? You're having a 99 with a flake. Sorted. Concentrate on a single idea and you will get that idea across. Dilute your message, the idea will be lost.

How to make sure your message gets across

First, identify the key element of your message. Then, here's a little trick to help you. Write a line that summarises your main idea. Leave a space and then write the line again. In the case of this chapter, the line is 'stick to one idea'. Then, between the two identical lines, just write what you want to write. Get your ideas down on the page.

Normally, when writing, you'll find you tend to move away from the key element of your message. Everyone does it. I do it as much as the next person. But by having that key element there below every line you write, you find that you can't get away from it! It forces you to think about each sentence and paragraph you write and question if it is relevant to the main point you're trying to get across. Be strict with yourself. Don't let your thought process wander and you'll find that whatever it is you're writing gets your message across much more effectively. And when you reach the end of the piece, if you've successfully harnessed the power of one, you'll have your natural conclusion.

Stick to one idea.

Top Tip

When it comes to generating ideas, I'm a big fan of a technique I picked up from writer and entrepreneur, James Altucher. James argues that the brain is like any other muscle and you need to exercise it. To do this he recommends you keep a notebook handy and every day you jot down at least ten ideas. They can be completely random, related to stuff you're working on or anything else that pops into your head. This daily routine helps to keep your brain active and, if you write down ten ideas a day, by the end of the year you should have 3,650 ideas. At least one of those ideas is bound to be good, and hopefully many more besides.

Part Two

Writing Copy

Chapter Six
Features Versus Benefits

"Ask the one question that's constantly at the forefront of your customer's mind: What's in it for me?"

— **Clayton Makepeace, American copywriter**

A key copywriting skill you must develop

Whenever training a new copywriter, one of the tasks I always set is a test to see whether the writer is able to turn features into benefits.

On the face of it, it seems a very simple exercise. Frankly, it is. But it reveals something about a writer that very quickly shows me if they have a skill I've found to be almost inherent in successful copywriters. This is the ability to understand the advantage of benefits over features when it comes to selling any product or service. You see, I ask all potential interviewees to write a 500-word piece of copy that attempts to sell me either a suit or an HB pencil. Doesn't sound too difficult, does it? It's not really. In fact, most people do it in a very similar way. Instances of the task being handled in a truly original way are few and far between.

But that's not the point. Really I'm looking for one thing – does the writer rely solely on features to sell to me, or is there some evidence that, on a subconscious level at least, they're thinking about the benefits those features might afford me. It's incredibly interesting to see how people handle it and you'd be surprised how well it works as a litmus test for how successful a trainee copywriter could become.

But hey, you've heard it before, right? This talk of features and benefits? It's a copywriting concept that goes back decades. You'll find it discussed in books by David Ogilvy, by Eugene Schwartz, as far back as Claude Hopkins too. You go to any copywriting event today and you should see it on the agenda. If you don't, ask for your money back. Seriously. This is copywriting 101 stuff. And sure, it's obvious. But my God, it's so **absolutely essential** that it's worth discussing on a regular basis. In fact, if you only ever learn one thing about copywriting... learn the importance of using benefits over features.

I can hear you shouting "I've got you, Glenn. I've got you. I already got it covered, man." If you have, great. Still, I'd rather be safe than sorry. Just in case. I mean, call me paranoid, but I can't help pick up sales letters, glimpse at Facebook ads and drive past billboards on a regular basis and notice features being used to sell instead of benefits. Someone out there isn't getting the message.

The eternal difference between features and benefits

For those ruffians at the back, let us look at exactly what the difference is between features and benefits, and then we'll also look at something you can do to make your benefits even more effective.

Let's take the pencil as an example...

One feature of a pencil is that it has a graphite nib. One benefit of such a feature is that you can easily erase any mistakes you make. This is harder to do with an ink pen. Even in this basic example you can already see that describing a benefit makes the pencil immediately more attractive to a potential buyer. It's not rocket science, you're just making life easier for the customer: rather than having to figure out the benefit themselves (and therefore running the risk they might not figure it out), you spell out the benefit. Simple. And indeed, that's the minimum you must do when it comes to copywriting – turn features into benefits. But there's much more you can do.

Charge your benefits with an emotional narrative

Now, the fact you can easily erase your mistakes is a benefit, but it's still not the easiest thing for a customer to connect with. Often basic benefits like this are things we take for granted. So, to really connect with potential customers, you need to take your benefits to another level. You need to charge them with an emotional narrative.

In our example, you might speak about the day of an exam and the fact that the student has been studying for this moment all year. As the clock ticks down, the student sits back and relaxes, happy they've completed the exam. They start to imagine life after this, all the things they'll achieve. But suddenly they panic! They remember question four and realise they've marked the wrong answer. There are only a few seconds left, but thanks to the fact they used a pencil... the student is able to quickly erase it and rewrite the correct answer!

A week later the student is celebrating in a bar having received their results that morning. They scraped the highest grade by a single mark; the answer they were able to erase and correct made all the difference.

It's a crude example, but you can see what I mean. The little old feature has come a long way, right? Originally it was just a graphite nib, but now it's the difference between grades on an exam. People rarely buy features. But neither do they always buy benefits. What people really want to buy are narratives. I mean, you don't buy a Maserati just because it has a powerful engine (a feature), nor do you really buy it because it's fast (a benefit). Most sports cars are fast. No, people buy a Maserati because – for them – it's charged with an emotional narrative of wealth and success.

When it comes to your own copy, make sure you're not trying to sell something on its features alone. Think about the benefits those features will afford the customer and sell them on those instead. Once you've got that sorted and you feel comfortable with your benefits, try to charge them with an emotional narrative. Think beyond the benefit alone. Ask yourself how that benefit could change someone's life. Do that and you'll soon see your copy stand out above everyone else's.

Always turn features into benefits

Below I've detailed ten items. For each, I'd like you to jot down a feature and a benefit. It shouldn't be too tough. This is just to get a basic understanding so you can quickly see how a feature can be improved by turning it into a benefit. Don't rush, and if you can, try to think of more obscure examples to test your knowledge.

Item	Feature	Benefit
A can of coke		
A running shoe		
A pint of beer		
A calculator		
An iPhone		
A bar of chocolate		
A holiday in Spain		
A £10 note		
An ice cream		
A book of fiction		

Top Tip

If you're writing copy for a product or service you don't often use or aren't familiar with, don't just rely on your own interpretation of it. Sure, it's possible to draw out some benefits yourself, but you'll be able to tap into much more interesting and authentic benefits if you speak to people who do use the product or service. They might hit upon a small detail you wouldn't have naturally thought about. But that tiny detail might be the one thing that really hits home and helps other potential customers relate to the product or service on a deeper level.

Chapter Seven
Promise, Picture, Proof and Push

"Patterns are everywhere in nature."

— *Max Cohen, character from the film* π

The hidden structure in all good copy

Have you seen the film π? It's a mathematical thriller! Seriously. It's directed by Darren Aronofsky, who's a bit crazy anyway (see *Black Swan*, or more recently *Mother!*). In this film, the main character is basically trying to find a pattern behind the stock market. He believes the answer somehow lies in the figure π. You know, the 3.14 thing. Anyway, the guy pretty much drives himself mad trying to find a structure in something that isn't really there.

That's the thing with patterns. It's very difficult to find ones that are totally and utterly universal. Often there'll be anomalies and if you're not willing to accept that, you can go mad trying to iron them out. The less insane among us accept that there is some drawback to sticking resolutely to formulaic patterns and dump them when the time comes, but until those anomalies present themselves, it can be pretty useful to follow a certain pattern.

That's how I feel about the Four Ps. Don't get me wrong, the structure they present is not foolproof by any means. But when I was starting out, this was one of the very first concepts of direct-response copywriting that I learned and it's served me well. So, it makes sense that I share it with you here. First, though, I guess I should explain what the Four Ps are.

Introducing the Four Ps

As with all theories of copywriting, it depends who you ask. But I was always taught that direct copywriting greats Bill Bonner and Mark Ford came across this pattern when they set to analysing all the successful pieces of long copy they'd been producing in the 1980s. I've heard elsewhere it was prolific copywriter Bob Bly who came up with these. Others say it was my good friend and the first apprentice of Bill and Mark – a guy called John Forde. It doesn't really matter.

The point is that a lot of copywriting loosely follows this structure. First the writer makes a promise. Then they paint a picture. Following that, they provide proof of the promise and picture. And finally, they push the reader to take action. In rough theory, the picture and proof are the biggest sections. Obviously, the more proof you're able to pile into your copy, the more likely someone will be persuaded to click and take action. In theory at least.

A very rudimentary way of looking at this structure would be something like this:

Promise
Picture
Proof
Push

It's a simple formula – but a strong one. In recent years, I've come to realise that this can be used on a much more focused level, which I'll explain in a little while. First, I'd like to take a moment to look into why each of these elements are so important.

Promise: The simplest way to get a reader's attention

Later in the book, when we look at headlines and leads, you'll see that there are actually several different ways you can get a reader's attention. But making a promise is a simple classic, and I guess that's why it made it into the Four Ps. It makes sense, right? When someone makes you a bold promise you're going to want to find out more. Who wouldn't? And promise headlines have worked well for years. Still do.

With financial copy, I'm sure you've come across many headlines promising that if you buy stock Y you could make X gain. And in health copy you'll have no doubt come across a new vitamin supplement that promises to reduce arthritic pain. As I say, promise-type headlines are very much the bread and butter of direct-response copy.

But, at a copywriting conference in the US, I was interested by a little nugget of advice – shared by copywriting legend, Bob Bly – that added a new dimension to promise-type headlines. Bob briefly spoke about promise-type headlines and covered the usual advice: they should be bold, they should be specific and – as much as possible – they should be unique. Sure, it's all good advice, but he went on to speak about a "secondary promise". This is what caught my attention.

You see, Bob argued that when making a big promise in your headline, you should follow it up straightaway with a subhead that contains a secondary promise. And he suggested this secondary promise should be smaller than the promise you make in your main headline. Initially you might think this undermines your big promise. But in actual fact, that is far from the case.

If you do it right, this secondary promise can make your whole headline a lot more effective. For example, your big promise might be something like:

> "If this penny stock company secures its patent on April 14th you could make a 500% gain overnight on every share you buy today."

All well and good and a speculative investor might be sold on that. But applying Bob's theory, think about what would happen if you followed that big promise with something like:

> "But even if it fails to get the patent, you could still make 50% over the next 12 months."

Now you can't lose. If the big promise delivers you make money, but even if it doesn't you still make money. For the reader it's a win-win situation and you've pretty much sold them in the first few lines of your copy.

The key to using this secondary promise is ensuring that the promise you make is smaller than the one you make in the main headline, whilst still making sure it contains a benefit that would make the reader want to purchase what you're selling.

Picture: Putting the reader in the action

Engaging with your audience is one of the most important skills you can learn when writing direct-response copy. Painting a picture for the reader is one way of doing exactly that. But for some strange reason, a lot of people seem to think the world of work, the business world, should be a grey, lifeless place that exists between nine and five. People assume that you're not allowed to be interesting, that you have to talk in facts and figures and graphs – you know: all the boring stuff. I see so much copy that is so dry, so void of life that I wonder if robots wrote it.

By contrast, the most successful copywriting often has a story element to it, some form of narrative that is engaging and entertaining – that makes you want to read more. Your message will be communicated so much more effectively if you focus your attention on working an engaging story into your message.

Take a look at this example:

> "Imagine yourself wearing a top hat and tails, on the balcony of a private rail car, the wind whistling past you as you sip the finest French champagne...

"It's 1850; the railroad is growing like a vine towards the west. And, although you don't know it yet, the same rail that you are riding on today will soon more than triple your wealth, making you and your family one of the great American dynasties..."

Good, isn't it? That's the opening two paragraphs of one of the most successful pieces of long copy ever. The copy, known by its headline of 'A New Railroad Across America', was written by Porter Stansberry, a master at using pictures to engage potential customers.

I think it would be useful, in fact, to give you a few more of the most effective examples of stories being used to engage a potential customer. We've seen Porter's historical railroad story. Now let's take a look at this one...

"You look out your window, past your gardener, who is busily pruning the lemon, cherry, and fig trees... amidst the splendour of gardenias, hibiscus, and hollyhocks.

"The sky is blue. The sea is a deeper blue, sparkling with sunlight.

"A gentle breeze comes drifting in from the ocean, clean and refreshing, as your maid brings you breakfast in bed.

"For a moment, you think you have died and gone to heaven.

"But this paradise is real. And affordable. In fact, it costs only half as much to live this dream lifestyle... as it would to stay in your own home!"

This legendary headline was used to launch *International Living* magazine. Though it was written by Bill Bonner many years ago, it's still one of the most successful ever promotions for the magazine. It's a great picture. It puts you right there in the story itself. It's your story, your window, your beautiful view. Straight off the bat you're engaged and arrested by the image and you want to read on. It's a great example.

Of course, both of the examples so far – to varying degrees – place you in the story. But it's not always necessary. It is possible to engage your reader with an entirely third person narrative, as was done in this famous *Wall Street Journal* promotion:

"On a beautiful late spring afternoon, twenty-five years ago, two young men graduated from the same college. They were very much alike, these two young men. Both had been better than average students, both were personable and both – as young college graduates are – were filled with ambitious dreams for the future.

"Recently, these men returned to their college for their 25th reunion."

You're not involved in this story, but it's still engaging. Reading about the two young men who were so alike and are now meeting again 25 years later, you want to find out what's happened.

These are just three examples – there are many more. But three particular factors unite them, which put into practice will help you enormously in developing your own writing.

First, as evidenced in Bill Bonner's great example, the story must be specific to detail: "…busily pruning the lemon, cherry, and fig trees." It's the little details that people recognise and relate to and real details like that bring the story to life.

Second, the story must naturally flow and relate to your message. You can be inventive, of course, but the underlying link must be valid. Stansberry's railroad story was all about new developments, era-defining developments that some people used to become rich. His message continued along those lines, revealing the era-defining developments he believed were afoot.

Third, and for me most important: throw the reader straight into it. Where possible start in the middle of the story. Sometimes, a little background might be necessary but keep it to a minimum. Remember, a little mystery is often what's so engaging about a story – you read on to find out what happens.

Proof: Make sure you're not just blowing smoke

It's all well and good using artful copywriting techniques to convince someone to click and buy something from you, but without some kind of proof, you're setting yourself an uphill struggle. It goes without saying that any accomplished piece of copy will contain within it an element of proof.

There are many types of proof that you can use, such as the performance of the product or service, testimonials from people who have already been using it, or anecdotal proof and logical proof. If you've got a good bucket of research you should have:

- **Newspaper quotes** – These are headlines from online or offline news outlets that reiterate the idea. For example, if you're writing about the Bank of England raising rates, if you have the *Times* saying "The Bank of England plan to raise rates," it's going to lend weight to your argument.

- **Case studies** – If you can show that what you're saying will happen to the reader has already happened to people in real life, then this will lend further support to your argument.

- **Testimonials** – When it comes to making promises, if you can back those promises up with quotes from existing readers who've already realised those promises…you're on to a winner.

- **Past performance** – It will pay to be able to show how the product or service has worked in the past. Examples of previous results can be very powerful and showing them, rather than just telling someone they did happen, will help increase response.

Recently I've also seen some really good use of social media as proof in a number of current sales letters. If one of the people you're writing about is on Twitter, look for a tweet that backs-up your argument and include a screenshot of it in your copy.

It's important to remember that when it comes to dealing with proof, you can never really have too much of it, so you need to get hold of as much as you can. This comes from research, digging into the product or service, and finding out as much about it as you can. Thanks to the internet this is a lot easier than it used to be.

We're working here in the world of direct-response, so once you've made a promise, painted a picture and provided enough proof, you need to make sure people act upon your copy.

Push: Getting the nod

You know that feeling when you read something you agree with and you start nodding? Even though you're just reading words on a page, the author has written something that strikes such a chord, you can't help but crack a wry smile, nod along and think, "Yeah, I thought that too." Do you ever get that? You do, right? Maybe even now you're nodding along reading this, thinking, "Yeah, that does happen to me."

Hmmm. That's interesting. In fact, it's downright bloody useful. You see if you can get readers nodding along with you when they're reading your copy, they'll be far more inclined to continue nodding in agreement when you ask for a click, or even the sale. Of course, it's hardly rocket science. I mean, it figures that if you agree with the author on one thing, you're more likely to agree with him on other things too. Including the fact that he thinks you should buy his product. You agree? Huzzah.

This idea can be used in a powerful way when it comes to the push section of your copy. I've used it many times – actually, thinking about it, I've probably done it in one form or another in every major piece of copy I've written. A piece of copy I wrote many years ago features this snippet:

"Before I leave the house in the morning, I have a bit of a routine.

"Once I'm out of bed, I stretch out the sleep. I keep promising myself I'll do a little exercise at this point, but never seem to get round to it.

"More likely, I'll wander into the kitchen, fill up the kettle, chuck a spoonful of coffee in a mug and then wander over to the curtain to take a peak outside.

"Do you do that too? Check the weather each morning? I don't know if I'm ever expecting anything special, like sun or snow... it's usually just the usual grey English morning."

That last bit, about checking the weather outside, is something you can imagine most people doing, right? And so the reader relates to it and starts nodding.

Now this letter is designed to sell a currency trading strategy and you might wonder how all this 'checking the weather' nonsense is relevant? Well, it does tie in to the product a little, but that's not why I chose to include it. This is in the letter to make people nod. Simple as that. And it is a physical reaction you should be aiming for here, an actual nod.

To do this you first need to find something that you know the reader will relate to and agree with. Ideally you want an accepted truth, i.e. you know two plus two is four, right? The scenario I used above is a little risky as not everyone will relate to what I'm talking about. But because it's a slightly more obscure reference, when a reader does relate, it'll be in a much stronger way. It should get the nod.

When trying this yourself, you should try different scenarios and test them with people in the office, or anyone who's around at home who you can ask. Once you've hit upon something people will relate to and agree with, you're almost there. Now, to give yourself the best chance of a nodding reader, you need a prompt. Notice in the extract above I directly ask the reader a question: "Do you do that too?" I did the same in the opening of this section. I asked: "Do you ever get that?" Then actually offered a response: "You do, right?"

These questions are consciously asked to prompt the reader into a nod. Obviously your reader isn't going to answer aloud; instead their brain will signal agreement in some other way, e.g. a nod.

Hurrah! You've now used your copy to engineer an unconscious physical reaction in the reader that will help influence their decision to buy. Good stuff. The key is to get your reader agreeing with you about something and for that agreement to manifest itself physically. Remember, it doesn't necessarily need to be an agreement on a point that relates to the product or service you're selling – this isn't about the product, it's about your reader and your attempt to persuade them.

And there you have it: the Four Ps in a nutshell. Before we move on, I'd like you to spend a little more time thinking about the Four Ps, so I've set a specific task for you to have a go at.

Spot as many Ps as you can

Earlier I mentioned that I've come to realise that the Four Ps can be used in a much more focused way, not just for the general structure of a long copy sales letter. You see, when you start to analyse long copy you notice that little bits of promise, picture, proof and even push are dotted throughout. This is interesting. In fact, from the research I've done into successful direct-response copy, I've seen a trend that the best copy constantly cycles through these four elements – sometimes as often as every few paragraphs.

No doubt you can see why this works. By constantly repeating these elements you reaffirm the ideas in the mind of the reader so that they are reminded of the promise, the picture you've painted for them, the different elements of proof you've shared, and a reminder that to get hold of the product or service you're selling, at the end of the copy, they will need to act.

One piece of copy that evidences this well is the copy guide sales letter I asked you to copy out by hand. Indeed, it's this letter I would like you to read through again to find as many instances of the Four Ps being used as possible.

Read through the piece again and wherever you spot a promise, a picture, a piece of proof or push, make a note next to it. Eventually, you'll find that almost every paragraph should have one of the Ps next to it. Indeed, you could argue that any paragraphs that are left without a P next to them are almost redundant. This is an interesting point and you should examine those paragraphs and ask – why are they included? It could be because they fulfil some other function, relating to one of the other aspects of good copywriting that is covered in his book. Alternatively, it could be they are extraneous and should be deleted.

Top Tip

The structure of the Four Ps is pretty universal, but it's not fixed in stone. Sometimes, to invigorate a piece of copy, you need to break the rules. If you find a piece of copy isn't quite hitting the mark, try leading with a picture or a piece of proof, instead of leading with the promise. Providing the key elements are all still included, mixing up the structure of how you present it could be just what that particular piece of copy needs to engage the customer.

Chapter Eight
Urgent, Useful, Unique and Ultra-Specific

> *"We're a what business, not a why business."*
>
> — **Bill Bonner, founder of The Agora**

A history of good copywriting

One of my mentors, the American entrepreneur and writer Mark Ford, once taught me a simple way to improve problematic headlines in copy. Many people have written about the idea many times before, so I thought rather than regurgitating it, I'd test it live, as I write this chapter. Why not, eh? It'll work like this: I'm going to pluck three promotions at random from Clickbank and see if we can't use this old school technique to quickly improve them. But first, let me just make sure we're both on the same page and explain to you the idea behind the Four Us.

A very potted history for you. One story goes: many years ago, Mark Ford and his business partner and copywriting legend, Bill Bonner, cobbled together all of the direct mail promotions they'd been sending out and studied which worked and which didn't. As they did with the Four Ps we looked at in the previous chapter, they noted the similarities and highlighted the differences in both those that worked and those that didn't. Then, after much hard slog and various analytical tests (that we'll skip over here for the sake of time)… Boom. They uncovered four elements that were consistently present in all of the most successful headlines.

What were they?

Drum roll, please.

First, each headline created a sense of **urgency**. Second, each headline offered something **useful**. Third, each headline contained something **unique**. And finally, each headline was **specific**. Er... hold on. Hold on. Let's try that again... And finally, each headline was **ultra-specific**. I know. I know. The last one has been tweaked a bit to bring it into line and it's not strictly a U. But it does make it easier to remember.

Regardless, it's an extremely helpful idea that you will do well to learn. Because if you're ever struggling to understand why a piece of copy isn't working as well as it should, chances are it's because you're missing one of these four elements. Make sense? Of course it does. Let's put it to the test on three headlines I selected at random from Clickbank promotions...

Putting the Four Us to the test

6.52pm, The Roundhouse, Wandsworth: First of all, I just searched for the term 'internet marketing' and the first product I hit at random is a coaching program. The headline on the sales page is a great example of something that's lacking the vast majority of the Four Us. Here it is. Seriously...

> # "FINALLY LEARN HOW TO MAKE MONEY ONLINE!"

I know you're looking at that and you've already realised it's obscenely generic and a tiny bit rubbish. But let's work through the four…

1. **Urgency**: There is none. Simple. Really, there's no need to go on here. There is no urgency in that headline. An immediate improvement could be "Finally, learn how to make money online TODAY!" It's still crap, but the simple addition of 'today' has already made it seem more urgent.

2. **Useful**: Almost all headlines have some form of usefulness – especially when they contain a monetary promise – so this is always a tough one. But when you think about it, if you have no knowledge of what 'online' means, how useful is this headline to you? Not very. Let's make it more so: "Finally, learn how to make money TODAY, even if you're struggling to pay the bills." Here we've immediately associated the monetary benefit with something that would be useful to everyone.

3. **Unique**: This headline is not unique. A quick improvement: "Finally, how a 15-year-old Aztec code could unlock the secret to making money online TODAY." Complete nonsense, but you get the point – a unique element makes it far more intriguing.

4. **Ultra-specific**: Where the uniqueness of a headline is looking for it to say something new, when it comes to being more specific, you're looking to include details that make your headline more authentic. Our example here is not in any way specific. Improve it thus: "Finally, a simple six-week program that reveals how to make £2,000 a month from online affiliate marketing." That's the same as the original headline – just more specific.

OK. That was an easy one. But it did allow us to quickly see the basic principles of the Four Us in action.

7.12pm, The Roundhouse, Wandsworth: Here I've picked another promotion at random searching for 'financial trading'. It's still a terrible headline and looks like it was designed by a mouse that's been sniffing too much cheese. But to be fair, it's a much better effort than our last example. Let's break it down using the Four Us…

Swing Traders, Spread Betters & Investors...

Copy my trading strategy and you could be making **consistent profits**............ month in, month out!

STARTING NOW!

Whether the market is going **UP** or **DOWN**

Years of research, testing and trading finally paid off! And it's all in my book

Short Swing Trading

for **YOU** to **PROFIT** from!

Whether you are:

New to trading

Or an experienced trader

...you will learn to use my **comprehensive and complete** trading strategy to get returns like this...

1. **Urgency**: See that "STARTING NOW"? Well, it's obvious the writer of this is on the right lines. That does create a little more urgency than the last headline. But it's still pretty rudimentary. Real urgency is usually created in two ways: either through a limited access play (e.g., only 500 people will get to use this) or by finding a genuine detail in the concept surrounding the product that provides a natural sense of urgency (e.g., a penny

share that's waiting for a big company announcement in the next few days). An improvement here could be to add details of a major news announcement that's due in the next few days or weeks that could provide a great opportunity to use the swing trading strategy.

2. **Useful**: Again, they've had a go at this here. That little section on "Whether you are…" is a good nod to expanding the usefulness of this headline. As I say, the use of a product or service is often inherent when you're making a monetary promise. I can't criticise too much here.

3. **Unique**: As for this headline being unique, I'm less forgiving. If you've never seen a financial system type headline before, it might seem unique, but I assure you it's actually pretty damn bland. Copy my strategy… doesn't matter which direction the markets are moving… no experience needed. It's all bland, overused stuff. An improvement? I'd like to see more development of the 'short' idea. Swing trading strategies are two-a-penny, but what is it about short swing trading that is so good? A starting point for a better headline: "Revealed: The simple mistake every swing trader makes on a daily basis and how avoiding it could make you £500 a day."

4. **Ultra-specific**: Again, on the face of it, this looks like it's ticking the boxes, but look again. Consistent profits, the market, month in, month out, years of research and testing. It's all utterly vague. It alludes all over the shop. Alluding is not good. It's bad. Consistent profits? Detail them. The market? Which market? Month in, month out? How much can I expect a month? Years of research and testing? Since when have you been testing? More detail please. If you've done the work – tell me about it.

Again, you can see that following the Four Us allows you to ask the right questions about a headline and find problems that you might not have seen at first glance. Let's have a look at one more example.

7.37pm, The Roundhouse, Wandsworth: Ha. Now, when I searched for the word 'health' and landed on this page, my first reaction was to pick another example. But I won't cheat – let's have a look at it…

Ever wondered what the Bible has to say about your health and what foods to eat in order to prevent cancer, heart disease, diabetes and high blood pressure?

God spoke about His Health Laws in the books of Deuteronomy, Exodus and Leviticus. Haven't you read?

To avoid inadvertently causing any offence, let me first say that I'm not religious myself, but I respect those that are. That said – beliefs aside – this is actually quite a good headline…

1. **Urgency**: It fails here. There's not really any obvious urgency. More and more, I realise that one of the most important questions you can ask of a headline is: why should I listen now? Aside from the inherent urgency generated from the health issues mentioned, there's no reason to buy *now*. I'd improve this by looking to change that "Haven't you read?" line and adding a simple "Read on before it's too late for you and your family." It's harsh, but seems fitting with the general feel of the piece.

2. **Useful**: This is useful despite not having a monetary claim. Instead it has the implied use of helping to prevent a number of awful diseases. I would be tempted to make this implied usefulness more explicit by altering the wording of the headline. You see, the problem with asking a question is that I could potentially answer: "No." But if you rephrased it and said "Discover how the Bible can show you which foods to eat to prevent, etc." I think it would be more effective.

3. **Unique**: Er… yeah, I'm not going to say this isn't unique. I've never seen a headline like this before. Fair play.

4. **Ultra-specific**: Again, pretty good job here. It's specific about the diseases. It's specific about the books of God that you should read to find out more. What can I say? The writer's done a good job with specificity. You find examples of good copy in the strangest places!

What to do if your copy isn't converting

In each of the headlines I selected, it's obvious that simple improvements can be made using the Four Us theory and in each case these changes make a big difference to how effective the copy is. Before I set about writing this chapter, I wondered if it might be harder to evidence the usefulness of the Four Us, but this random exercise just proves how universal they are and why you should spend some time thinking about them in regard to your own headlines.

If you're ever stuck with a headline that's not working as well as you hoped, look at it again and think about which of the Four Us it's missing.

Top Tip

Don't think about the Four Us until after you've written the first draft of your copy. Copywriting is ultimately a creative act and when it comes to creativity, I believe you should rely as much as possible on the strange cave of secrets that is your subconscious. That's often where the magic happens, so to speak. Once you've got the weird and wonderful contents of your imagination on the page, that's when you should apply concepts like the Four Us to your copy. Use them to direct, not dictate.

Chapter Nine
Writing Headlines

> *"I write the paragraph, then I'm crossing out, changing words, trying to improve it."*
>
> — **Paul Auster**

Live. Die. Repeat.

That's the tagline of the Tom Cruise movie, *Edge of Tomorrow*. Have you seen it? Basically Tom Cruise gets the blood of an alien on him, which means that whenever he's killed he returns to the day he got the alien blood on him. He meets Emily Blunt and then he has to save the world. A regular day at the office for Cruise. To be fair though, it's actually OK. In fact, when it was released and I went to see it at the cinema, I was inspired to sit in a café to write this very section of the book right after. It just goes to show how random input from films, books and music can help inspire ideas – a thought we looked at earlier.

That tagline gave me the opening I needed to talk about my approach to writing headlines and subject lines. How come? You can summarize my headline approach like this: Write. Delete. Repeat.

See what I've done there?

The good news is, when you adopt this approach to headline writing, there's no risk of being attacked by time-warping, matrix-like aliens. Or Tom Cruise. How does this 'Write. Delete. Repeat.' approach work and – more importantly – why does it work?

Write: Give quantity a chance to find quality

It's almost impossible to write a headline in one sitting. In my experience, when it comes to finding a good headline, quantity leads to quality. Your first words will always be a little loose, convoluted or – quite possibly – crap. Don't take it personally; few great ideas are born perfect. They must be shaped and molded, broken down and built back up. To do that in your brain is very difficult. Plus, it's counter-intuitive.

Remember, ultimately people will be reading your headline on the page or screen. How your words look is just as important as what they say. Some words sound clear in your mind but are hard to read. They just aren't right visually. That's why it's important you don't try to conceive your headline entirely in your head. You have to write. But of course, if you write the first idea you have, it probably won't be too sharp. Don't worry about that. Just write. Get your first idea down on the page and then...

Delete: Why you must conquer your fear of blank space

Get rid of it.

Really. Delete what you've written. It's no good. Or rather, if it is any good, you'll write it again in a moment. Just better.

Now, I know very well that deleting what you've written is hard. You're probably like me and assume every word you write is another drop of pure gold from the treasure trove that is your beautiful mind.

It's not.

I'm very much of the Hemingway school of writing and believe that writing is as much about crafting as it is conceiving. I see words and sentences as little blocks of wood that tumble onto the page. Once there, it's your job to pick them up and carve something from them. Something clean and clear and good. Was it Hemingway who said that he hoped he could write just one true sentence then he'd be happy? Something like that. With your headline, you should aim for the same.

And that's why, once you've written your first idea, you must take a knife to it (or the delete key, which causes less mess) and carve it up. Then…

Repeat: Nobody said it'd be easy

Repeat… and repeat… and repeat. And before you ask: yes, it is a slog. But you'll find that the process of writing a good headline is made much quicker if you accept that you're going to need to put some work in. You need to keep carving up your words until something good presents itself. If you try to avoid the work and conjure up a headline from thin air, you'll be stuck at your desk a lot longer than you need to be. Change the order, tweak minor words, use the synonym function in Word if you must. But whatever you do, keep trying new angles on the page until you hit upon something that shines.

There you have it: the 'Write. Delete. Repeat.' approach to writing headlines. Perhaps you already practice something similar. I hope so, it means you're already on the right lines. The key thing to remember is that you must be disciplined and willing to delete. Don't be precious with your ideas. Don't be overprotective of your words. Trust yourself to be better. Trust yourself to work harder. And trust yourself to craft a headline that will truly engage your reader. And when you do…

Delete it all and do it again!

Glove and Boots

I'm a huge fan of the 'Glove and Boots' blog. There are very few sites on the web that I actively visit to check for updates, but Glove and Boots is one of them. Sadly, they don't post as much these days, but there's a good archive of material. The reason I'm writing about them in this book is that in one of their videos, they very wisely point out that by overloading your headlines and subject lines with hyperbolic and misleading claims – otherwise known as clickbaiting – you'll eventually lose credibility.

That's one of the reasons I love the blog so much. Aside from catering to my love of Jim Henson-esque puppetry, the guys behind the blog are obviously pretty clued-up on internet marketing.

Hang on... puppetry?

Oh yeah, I forgot to mention Glove and Boots is a video blog presented by a Mario and Fafa. I'm not sure what animal Mario is, but Fafa is definitely a groundhog. You should search for their stuff on YouTube. It's a lot of fun, but there is a serious lesson to be learned when it comes to getting that all-important click.

As Fafa points out in one of the videos, if you overload your headlines or subject lines with too much hyperbole and don't pay off in the content itself, you're going to create a sense of distrust between you and your reader. This is bad. Of course, it's not to say you shouldn't attempt to write engaging and attention-grabbing headlines, you definitely should. But using cheap proclamation tactics like "the best thing you'll ever see..." or "the most profitable way to..." will only cause a negative response unless it's really true.

Indeed, an email landed in my inbox just yesterday inviting me to the UK's most popular two-hour seminar on cryptocurrencies. Totally unquantifiable, of course. And ultimately, just bad copy. There are many ways to cause intrigue and excitement in a headline, without hyperbole.

No need for hyperbole

Looking through the most popular subject lines from my own email newsletter (which you can register for at AllGoodCopy.com), you can see that a successful headline doesn't need to blow smoke. Here's three top performers:

"Back from my travels with a brand new free guide" – I was surprised by this myself as it's very literal and almost a bit boring. But perhaps it ranks highly for that very reason. It offers something free that is then provided in the content and has intrigue because you wonder where my travels have taken me and what the free guide could be. No nonsense here, it's just simple and relevant.

"Say hello to a more imaginative salutation in your copy" – Again, nothing really promised here and certainly no hyperbole or emotional manipulation – just a soft play on the word salutation. Indeed, the piece was all about salutations in copywriting and by focusing on the content, the headline paid off.

"Did this hard-working piece of copy really kill JFK?" – Now, this is veering towards clickbait. But I think it redeems itself by referencing the content too. If the subject line had been "Proof who killed JFK" anyone who opened the email expecting to see the president's shooting from a different angle would have been bitterly disappointed to find an article about eyebrows (a mini-headline that precedes the main headline) in direct-response copy. Instead, what this subject line does is take the intrigue of a clickbait headline, but makes it relevant to the content by overtly stating that it has to do with copy.

You can see that it is OK to avoid hyperbole and misleading proclamations in your headlines, and if you signal your content appropriately, you can still enjoy the benefit of intrigue that a clickbait type headline would generate, without upsetting your reader and losing trust.

Disrupt. Intrigue. Engage.

What's the alternative to writing clickbait copy? Whether you're writing headlines for Facebook adverts, subject lines for emails, or just for flyers to hand out to strangers in the detergent aisle of your local grocery store, here's a technique for writing attention-grabbing headlines. It breaks down into three steps.

1. Disrupt

The first thing you need to do is disrupt the reader. This can be in the form of a statement, a promise, a claim, a question or an image. But it needs to be unexpected or out of the ordinary.

- Read This or Die Poor...

- Four Time Bomb Investments That Could Demolish Your Portfolio...

- Don't Risk Putting Another Pound In Your Bank Until You've Read This...

These are all great examples of disruptive headlines.

For this, you can use the Four Us as a guide. Is your headline unique? Is there any urgency? Does it offer some use to the reader? Is it ultra-specific? Make sure you can answer at least one or two of these questions to the positive and you shouldn't be too far off. As for the subject matter of your headline, you can find inspiration from two main sources: the copy a reader will reach if they click on your headline; or the reader who's reading your headline.

When it comes to taking inspiration from the copy, look to the details, even if it's something unique about the offer. The copy you're linking to should be full of subject matter for you to base your headline on. Above all, make sure you mix it up.

Let's say you're selling an advisory service about trading the financial markets. The idea behind the copy you're linking to – and the service itself – is all about how you could shave years off your retirement date by learning to trade the financial markets by following the advice shared in the service. You might find some people react better to a headline that focuses on a free gift you're giving away as part of offer. At the end of the day, some people just get excited about free gifts. But other people might be more attracted to the end result, the deeper benefit of what you're selling, i.e. the fact that you could shave years off your retirement age. Both angles are valid; you just need to test them to see which takes off and which appeals with which sections of your market.

When it comes to drawing inspiration from the reader, look to what they're reading about in the news or watching on television, or alternatively think about their personal needs and wants. To continue with our trading service example, you could look to reports in the news about people having to retire later in life. They're already seeing this story in the news and it's likely to be at the forefront of their mind, so when they see the reference to it in your advert's headline, it's going to be more disruptive. Alternatively you could try to tap into the fact that pretty much everyone wants to retire earlier.

Now you should have a disruptive element to your headline that relates directly to the copy you're trying to lead the reader to. By far this is the most important part, so spend the most time here. If you're just looking to write a new subject line, you can stop here. But if you need a longer headline, the next step is to add intrigue.

2. Intrigue

Once you've identified how to disrupt the reader, you need to flesh it out a little by adding another level of intrigue. You need to ask what is it specifically that makes it essential for the reader to find out more about this. And why. The key here is to make sure you don't wrongly interpret being intriguing as being vague. Though you want to keep the detail of the copy you're linking to a secret, you should still use specific language and imagery. You also need to keep things short and you shouldn't try to over explain things at this point. You don't need to add a lot more here. Just develop the headline with one or two more intriguing details.

For example, if your headline currently reads "Revealed: How To Get Paid Everyday..." you could make it more intriguing by adding something like: "Revealed: How To Get Paid Everyday Without Doing Any Extra Work". It's just about finding that extra little detail that makes people think "I've got to know what that is."

3. Engage

The final thing your advert must do is make the reader engage with you. This is critically important. No matter how disruptive or intriguing your headline is, if the reader doesn't engage and click, it's all for naught. You need to give clear guidance, incentive and reassurance to the reader so that it would be a mistake not to click. Let's break that down.

First, don't assume the reader knows to click. I know it seems obvious, but it's very possible you could be writing to an older market who isn't as internet-savvy as you might presume. Not just that, but from a design perspective adverts can often blend into editorial. Make a very clear call to action. But don't stop there. Make sure you also give an incentive for the reader to click. Don't just say "Click here to find out more". Instead, try "Click here and you'll receive the full details immediately". You need to make it obvious that the reader will get something – however small or seemingly incidental – for clicking.

Finally, if you really want to nail it, try to reassure the reader that it's a good idea to click the advert. Instead of "Click here and you'll discover the secret", try something like "Click here and you'll be thankful you finally discovered the secret". Again, it's a really small tweak, but it's just adding that extra emotional touch that will subconsciously give the reader that push to click. And once they've clicked, you're done. The advert has done its job. Hurrah. Remember all you need to do is: Disrupt. Intrigue. Engage.

The inbox battlefield

In any business, you'll likely spend a ton of your time trying to come up with original headlines for email subject lines to grab attention and get the click. It's hard work, right? Let me ask you, should you even bother? Especially when there's a way you can hijack existing subject lines – that are otherwise considered boring – and use them to far outperform anything original you might think up. Hmmm – that sounds interesting.

And get this. I've tested this on a number of occasions, to a responsive email list of over 65,000 opted-in subscribers, and each time this technique topped the stats for open rates. Plus, just so you know this isn't about getting the open and then losing attention immediately, or causing a spam issue: each time I've tested it, the click through rate (CTR) has been above average too.

Before I explain how you can use this particular type of 'boring' subject line to increase your open rate whilst maintaining a decent CTR, let me just point out something fundamental about subject lines. It's this: you must mix things up. Though this technique will see you hit some really high open rates, if you do it on every single email, your readers will begin to recognise what you're doing and dismiss your email messages.

Why you always open certain subject lines

What I'm suggesting here seems to go against natural thought – why would you hijack a boring subject line that is used all the time? The point is that there are *some* boring and essentially administrative subject lines that you almost always open; no matter how many times you see them. For example, how often do you open emails titled:

Your Order from Amazon.co.uk

Or, maybe:

Glenn, you have a Facebook notification pending

Or, even:

Glenn Fisher (@allgoodcopy) is now following you on Twitter!

Let me tell you, you open them *much more* than you realise. Sure, you tend to delete or file them away pretty quickly too – and with this technique the window to maintain someone's attention is very short. But as the clicks in my testing prove, it is possible.

Yes, using administrative subject lines like this works a treat for increasing the open rate of your emails. Fair play, though, I can already hear you thinking: how the hell am I going to lead on into my regular email by referencing a shipment notice from Amazon in my subject line?

To be honest, you're going to need to figure that one out for yourself depending on what business you're writing copy for. But I think everyone has content that can be topped with a subject line that utilises this technique in some way. Seriously, it just takes a little clever thinking.

For the Amazon one, I was writing for a guide to second-hand selling on Amazon and began the email itself by explaining I was tired of seeing said subject line because it meant I'd spent even more money with them. I then went on to offer a way to actually make some money using Amazon. With the Facebook notification one – simple – I used that when the business I was writing for was contacting its customers about setting up a Facebook page.

Don't try to force it: this technique is just one option among many. It's one of those ideas that you just need to have floating around and then when the right moment crops up, you can smack this into action and bang, you'll see your open rate fly up.

Top Tip

Personalisation in headlines and subject lines works. Modern marketing techniques allow us to collect personal details about potential customers, such as their name. With that information, we can often address our readers personally. I'm sure you've received a message from a company with a subject line along the lines of: "Glenn, check this out."

I recently received a piece of copy that even had my dog's name, Pablo, in the headline. Seeing your own name in a headline, staring back at you (or your dog's name, for that matter) does get your attention. Of course it does. And this is why tests including an element of personalisation often outperform a more universal headline.

But. And it's a big 'but'. I implore you to use the technique sparingly. The more often personalisation is used, the more noticeable it becomes. Your reader will soon start to associate the jarring personalisation with your emails. When this happens, the personalisation turns from being an effective tool to an annoying and cynical trick. My advice is to use personalisation when there is a genuine personal reason for getting in touch with the potential customer. That way, it will remain an authentic tool and you'll get the best results each time you do choose to use it.

Chapter Ten
Grabbing and Holding the Reader's Attention

"Marketing is a contest for people's attention."

— Seth Godin

A headline isn't just a headline

Any copywriter or marketer worth their salt will tell you: if you want copy to be successful, you've got to have a great headline and lead. That big idea up top that grabs attention and gets people excited and open-minded about the opportunity you're telling them about. In fact, a lot of pros will tell you to spend 80% of your time on the headline and lead and just 20% on the rest of the copy. I kind of just did myself.

But there's a problem with this idea. You see, chances are the headline and lead you're using right now is pretty much pointless. I read so much copy where it's obvious that the writer has spent a lot of time nailing that killer headline and lead. And in some cases, they've done it very well. As a reader, you want to continue reading, you want to find out more. So, job done.

But then something happens. The writer suddenly loses all their ability. As the copy goes on, it seems they've started taking drugs. They forget about the headline and lead. It's as though it never existed.

There's no point putting all your effort and energy in that great idea up front if you're not going to repeat it constantly. Constantly? Isn't that overkill? No. Definitely not. What's better? Coming up with a load of new angles and complicating your promotion with lots of different ideas, or sticking to that one core idea and referring back to it over and over again? Seriously. You might have heard of Malcolm Gladwell's book *The Tipping Point*. Well, that whole book is about this. Restating the core idea over and over and over.

It's so important to the success of any piece of copy that the main promise, the main claim, is repeated throughout – that it is kept constantly in the mind of the reader. You should be checking that the promise or claim made in the headline and lead is repeated at least once on every single page – minimum. And I'm not talking about repeating it in clever, ever abstracting ways. I'm talking about repeating that promise verbatim.

If you've promised returns of X, Y and Z in the headline, repeat those exact amounts. If you've used an analogy up top, use the exact same analogy throughout. If you put a time frame on it, use the same time frame throughout. If you're lucky, you'll probably be able to just copy and paste the headline when you need to restate it. But if it does jar the flow of the narrative and you need to change it slightly, just be sure you don't edit out the key elements.

Believe me, if you do this, your sales will increase. In fact, get this right and they will increase dramatically. Putting this principle into action myself on one occasion helped increase the effectiveness of a promotion by over 15%... and on another occasion it enabled a promotion to gross £100,000 in just six days.

If you or the copywriter you've hired has written a breakthrough headline and lead, don't waste it by forgetting about it.

Stick to the script

Take a look at this note:

Stake - gold rush - unique
every page

1,000 into 15,000 forecast - greed/useful
4, 5, 7, 9, 11, 20, 22, 23

195 spaces - scarcity
11, 18, 36 added 21, 30

Wednesday 20th December - urgency
3, 13, 14, 33 added 24

Gold coin - greed/scarcity
28, 29, 37 added 12

Map with stake - unique
1 added 11

From your couch - ease of use
2, 4, 11, 16, 21, 22, 29, 33, 34

Though it might look like nonsense right now, I guarantee that it will help you shave hours off the time you spend reviewing and editing your copy. And it'll make your copy a damn sight more effective. It's almost too simple to follow. And it only takes about five minutes from start to finish. Sound interesting? Good. Let me show you what it's all about.

Now, there's an old concept in direct-response copywriting called the *golden thread*. If you've never heard of it before, it's pretty straightforward to figure out. It suggests that when it comes to a piece of long copy, you should make sure the same idea runs throughout the piece, from the headline all the way to the call to action. It speaks to the *power of one* idea in general advertising, that sticking to one message is more powerful than trying to deliver numerous messages. Makes sense, right?

But. Of course, there was going to be a but. The concept of the golden thread is a little high-level and conceptual for my liking. I'd like to go deeper. Sure, it makes sense that if you're selling a gold mining advisory service, for example, you wouldn't suddenly start writing about Elon Musk developing a super battery in Arizona. They're two different ideas: gold mining and renewable energy. The golden thread, you could argue, in a letter about the opportunity in gold mining needs to be about gold mining throughout the letter. Stands to reason. But on a practical basis, when it comes to writing long copy, is it enough to just focus on pulling that single golden thread tightly throughout, whilst leaving everything else random and bitty? The answer is: most definitely no. For longer pieces of copy to be effective you will have many more elements to it, or many more threads, which are just as important as the main idea. All of these different elements need to be weaved throughout the letter too. Here's how you do it.

Hopefully you're with me here. Personally I thought the previous 200 or so words there were a little cerebral. But to make up for that, here's a cold, hard example from a piece of long copy I worked on myself. To set the scene, I'll tell you the letter is all about the opportunity of investing in gold mining companies on the verge of discovering gold and other precious metals. The basic pitch of the letter – the golden thread – is about inviting people to "claim a stake in the world's biggest new gold rush." Throughout the letter, I need to make sure I've touched on that key idea on almost every page. But, when I came to write the headline for this particular piece, I added a lot more than just that basic pitch. Indeed, there were **six** additional elements I added in. They were:

1. A forecast of the gains the expert believes readers can make.

2. The number of limited places available on the service.

3. The date of the deadline for new members to join the service.

4. A promise of a genuine gold coin for the first 50 to respond.

5. A map showing where the reader would be claiming their stake.

6. Detail that you can do this from the comfort of your own couch.

Now, each of these elements is designed to add something to the headline complex, be it urgency, uniqueness, scarcity or ease of use. We covered these ideas in Chapter 8. For now, the key point I want you to take away and apply to your own writing is this: each of these elements should be individually threaded throughout the pages of copy that follows the headline. If it's mentioned in the headline complex, it needs to run through the entire copy. If it doesn't, it means you're either missing an opportunity to touch on a key sales element, or you're leaving your reader with unresolved questions – which is even worse. The good news: as I say, I've got a very simple and practical approach you can use to check you're pulling each of these multiple threads through the copy.

The aim of the game here is to make sure you've not only paid off the key elements you added to the headline, but that you revisit them throughout the copy. Here's my process:

First, get a sheet of paper and a pen. Easy.

Next, you need to take each of the key elements you added to the headline complex and boil them down to a word or phrase. Here's how I did it:

1. A forecast of the gains the expert believes you can make = the numbers '£1,000 and £15,000'.

2. Detail of the limited number of places available on the service = the phrase '195 spaces'.

3. Detail of the deadline for new members to join the service = the date 'Wednesday 20th December'.

4. Promise of a gold coin for the first 50 to respond = the phrase 'gold coin'.

5. A map showing where the reader would be claiming their stake = no specific word, but the image of the map itself.

6. Detail that you can do this from the comfort of your own couch = the word 'couch'.

Write those words or phrases down on your scrap of paper. Now, take the first word or phrase on your list and find every occurrence of it in your copy and jot down the page number it appears on. You can do this very simply in most word processors or online in Google Docs by selecting 'Edit' from the main menu and then 'Find'. Type in the word your searching for and it will highlight all instances. Once you've done that, it should look something like this:

Key element: 195 places, 11, 18, 36.

Do this for each of the key words or phrases you've identified. And you should end up with a scrap of paper that looks something like mine:

Stake - gold rush - unique
every page

1,000 into 15,000 forecast - greed/useful
4, 5, 7, 9, 11, 20, 22, 23

195 spaces - scarcity
11, 18, 36 added 21, 30

Wednesday 20th December - urgency
3, 13, 14, 33 added 24

Gold coin - greed/scarcity
28, 29, 37 added 12

Map with stake - unique
1 added 11

From your couch - ease of use
2, 4, 11, 16, 21, 22, 29, 33, 34

Once you've got that we can move to the final phase of this process. Now you have a list of the key elements used in your headline complex and a visual record of how often they appear in your copy. In my example, you can see that I've marked my golden thread idea (stake, gold rush) as appearing on 'EVERY PAGE'. I've been doing this copywriting lark for a while, so I tend to inherently stick to the golden thread. And you can see that I've also immediately ticked a few of the other elements off too. I've done this wherever I can see that the page numbers run pretty consecutively and there's not more than a three or four page gap between mentions. As you become more experienced, you'll naturally pull more and more of these key threads through your copy without thinking about it.

You'll also see that for some of the other key elements, I've circled them and marked a cross next to the number series. For example, by following this process, I found that after the headline, I'd only mentioned the urgency date on pages 3, 13, 14 and 33. There are some big gaps there, particularly between pages 14 and 33.

Here you should review the copy and look for places to repeat the key element that's missing. Of course, this comes down to your own judgement and there might already be too many elements in a section for you to add it easily. That was the case when it came to finding a place between page 3 and 13. I can live with that as there's lots of other elements at work in the copy. But that gap between 14 and 33 was just too big. That is much too long for the element not to be mentioned. So, I just found a place between there – on page 24 – to repeat it. I followed this same process for each of the elements that I'd not repeated in the letter, making sure to pay them off and pull them tight throughout the piece. All in all it took about five minutes.

Madness? Quite possibly. Obscenely logical. Naturally. But in seriousness, I think it's a great exercise for any writer to do when they've finished a first draft. This is a very simple and effective way of making sure you carry all the key elements of your headline complex throughout your copy and I guarantee it will make it more effective. When reviewing copy – and having my own copy reviewed – this is by far one of the biggest areas for error. Over such long pieces of copy and when you consider how many distractions we have around us when reading such a letter, it's important that readers are regularly reminded of the key elements that caught their attention in the first place. This process makes sure you do that.

Of course, before you can start pulling the rainbow thread nice and tight, you've got to actually write something. As I say, we'll get to that later in the book, but right now, I want to share some thoughts on how to start any piece of copy.

Why you should always open like Bob Dylan

"Pistol shots ring out in the barroom night.

Enter Patty Valentine from the upper hall.

She sees the bartender in a pool of blood,

Cries out, 'My God, they killed them all!'

Here comes the story of the Hurricane,

The man the authorities came to blame,

For somethin' that he never done.

Put in a prison cell, but one time he could-a been

The champion of the world."

So opens the song *Hurricane* by Bob Dylan. And what an opening! Pistol shots are ringing out... the bartender's in a pool of blood... everyone's dead! You've got to know what's going on, right? So he tells you: it's "the story of the Hurricane," a guy stitched up for "somethin' that he never done." And on top of that he could have been "the champion of the world." How come? What's the story here? You're in. The scene is set and you sure as heck want to know more.

Whatever you're writing – a song, a sales promotion, an email, a blog post, a newsletter article, a magazine piece – you should always open like Bob Dylan does here.

These days we just don't have the time. On top of that, so much is wrestling for our attention that most things get lost by the wayside. So when it comes to getting someone's attention with a piece of writing you need to do it straight from the off. Otherwise whatever comes after is lost. Two-hundred words in you could make the greatest claim in the world, you could reveal that the Queen is having an affair with Jonathan Ross, you could offer free money, you could share the formula for turning water into wine… it wouldn't matter: you lost your audience at 'hello'. Question is: how do you open strong and get your reader's attention? Well, there are a number of ways but my advice is this: start at the end!

Whatever your piece may be, write it as normal. Just get your thoughts down on paper. Don't worry about how you kick it all off. When you're done look over the piece again. Nine times out of ten, the point you make, the reason you're writing at all will be hidden at the end. It's no good there. No one's ever going to get to it. So copy it and stick it right up top where everyone can see it. Then it's just a case of linking that up to your original opening and you're done. You've just dramatically increased the amount of people who will continue to read your piece. Well done.

Sizzling sentences with your sausages

Who in their right mind thinks about sentence structure whilst they're having their sausage sandwich in the morning? Me. And here's something for you to think about. For a few moments after reading it, a reader remembers the end of a sentence. Just there you remembered "end of a sentence", right? And having now ended twice on the phrase "end of a sentence", it's really starting to stick in your mind. By subtly altering your sentences you can take advantage of this to reinforce the core theme of your copy.

Take a look at this sentence: "You could profit on a daily basis by sparing just ten minutes a day." The sentence ends on "ten minutes a day", which is fine if that's the core message of your promotion – the fact it takes just ten minutes a day. But what if elsewhere in your promotion you've been developing the idea that you can do this on a daily basis? Well, with a subtle change you can end the sentence such: "Sparing just ten minutes a day, you could profit on a daily basis." Now the thought the reader's mind lingers on for a moment longer is the "on a daily basis". Sure, it's subtle stuff. But it's little technical tweaks like this – together with all the other little tweaks you make – that give your copy a successful edge.

Lead the reader through your copy

Keeping your audience engaged is one of the most important skills you can learn. In any business, your audience are your potential customers. And to effectively communicate with them, to encourage them to do business with you, you have to be able to engage them for longer than a few seconds. Stories are one way of doing exactly that.

The most successful emails, sales letters and adverts so often have a story element to them, some form of narrative that is engaging and entertaining – that makes you want to read more. That's what gets the click.

Use subheads to inform your narrative

Copywriters aren't often too kind to subheads. In fact, most of the time subheads are treated as nothing more than punctuation. Indeed, one of the uses of subheads in longer copy is as punctuation. But it is just one use. There are many more. The fact is, having strong subheads throughout your copy can be the difference between copy that bombs and copy that sells. So, let's just take it as accepted that you need to spend longer on your subheads.

The question now is: what can you do to make them stronger? To really supercharge a piece of copy, your subheads should be as intriguing and exciting as your main headline. There's no reason why you should disregard the rules you follow in constructing a main headline when you tackle your subheads.

For example, if you use the Four Us (that dictate a headline should be useful, unique, urgent and ultra-specific, as we saw earlier) for your main headline then you should apply them to each of your subheads too. As an absolute minimum, each of your subheads should communicate at least one clear benefit to the reader. This will help for two reasons:

1. As a reader works their way through your copy they'll be motivated to carry on reading as they're clearly reminded of a particular benefit by a subhead.

2. For anyone who starts to skim your copy, the subheads will help recapture the reader's attention. After the initial work done by your main headline, a series of subheads acts as an attention-grabbing safety net.

There's also a third, indirect bonus to concentrating more on your subheads. It's more of a technical thing for your own benefit. If your subheads are detailed and benefit-driven, they can act as a kind of contents page for you to ensure that the thread of your copy is consistent and you've covered everything you intended to.

Overloading your subheads

When it comes to writing the main headline of your copy, you should ensure it is as lean and direct as possible. It needs to crystallise a single idea in the quickest and most efficient way possible. But with subheads, you can be a bit more relaxed.

You're aiming these subheads primarily at people who are losing interest (either skimmers or readers who are not totally engaged in the narrative of the body copy), so you need to make sure there's plenty of good stuff in there to recapture their attention and force them to read on. As well as an obvious benefit – providing a solution to a problem for example – you should also work into the subhead some secondary benefits. An example:

Say the product you're promoting is about reducing back pain, rather than a subhead that just says:

"How you could reduce back pain using this special heat pad…"

Add a second, third and even fourth benefit:

"Discover how this scientifically-proven heat pad can reduce your back pain all through the day – it's light, discreet and takes less than five minutes to start relieving the pain."

A crude example, sure. But you can start to see what I mean. The second version is a much stronger subhead that has much more chance of re-engaging a skimmer or helping along a reader who wants to know more but is losing interest.

Because there are a lot of things mentioned in this subhead that you want to find out about – the speed of relief, the scientific proof, it's discreetness – you're more likely to read on a bit further to get the answers.

Supercharging your subheads

Having focused more on the copy you're using for your subheads and having loaded them with benefits to grab the attention of anyone scanning your sales promotion… you're looking pretty good. But there's something else you can do to really power-up your promo.

You see, so far we've taken it for granted that your subheads signal what issues are going to be discussed in the body copy that immediately follows and that when those issues are resolved you'll punctuate the copy with a new subhead. Indeed, longer pieces of copy do tend to follow this pattern. Very successful pieces in fact.

But the most successful copy does something slightly different. Instead of resolving everything that's teased in the subhead in the copy that follows, leave one issue unresolved and deal with it after the next subhead (which in turn will tease something that isn't dealt with until after the next subhead, and so on). It works.

Remember the readers of your copy are wise. They read books. They watch films. They watch television. Their unconscious is trained to note things and keep a record of any unanswered questions until they can be checked off as the answer presents itself. By leaving an element of your subhead unresolved, you can tap into this natural thought process and engage the reader on a much deeper level.

Focusing more on your subheads won't make a bad piece of copy good, but applying these elements to an already decent piece of copy could make it great.

Top Tip

When writing any longer pieces of copy such as a blog post, sales letter or email, you need to consistently shock people into taking notice again. It's only natural your reader will start to get distracted, no matter how well written and engaging your copy may be. We live in a world of constant distractions. That's why it's important to regularly interrupt your reader to actively ensure they're still engaged. You can do this by breaking your copy up with exclamations such as 'Wait! Did you just read that right?' or 'What you'll read next will shock you!' Alternatively, well-chosen images relating to your copy can be effective, or a series of short, sharp bullet points can help draw a reader's attention back to your main copy.

Chapter Eleven

Salutations, Fellow Copywriter

> *"Email is very informal, a memo. But I find that not signing off or not having a salutation bothers me."*
> — *Judith Martin*

Don't just say hello

I'd like to talk about salutations, my good friend. Or should I say *fellow copywriter?* Perhaps *future copywriting master* would be better? Of course, this is my point. There are far more options when it comes to addressing a reader than the classic 'Dear Reader'. Sure, it's a small thing. But still, salutations are used for a reason and to overlook them is lazy. It's also a missed opportunity to kick off your copy well and make a stronger connection with your reader.

First then, let's just get clear on the actual role of a salutation. A salutation is often there to link the attention grabbing elements of copy to the main content. In an email it takes the reader from the subject line or headline to the body copy of the email. In a sales letter it indicates the start of the letter itself. You may even find a salutation in a short online advert where it is even more important that you use it in the most effective way. But wherever a salutation does appear, ultimately it alerts the reader to the fact that the message is aimed at them.

That's kind of interesting in itself if you think about it. There's a certain suspension of disbelief going on with any piece of copy – when was the last time you received a message from a relative with a 48-point headline and a subhead promising you riches beyond your wildest dreams? We often forget that readers are only too aware that we're selling to them. But the best advertising doesn't seem like advertising at all. And any way of personalising your copy can help a reader forget they're being sold to. If the idea behind the copy is compelling enough, once the headline has done it's job of grabbing attention, the reader will quickly shift gears, looking to engage with the copy in a deeper way. At this point of transition, a salutation helps guide the way.

Being polite is a waste of time

A traditional salutation reassures someone that they are reading a message from someone real, not just a piece of advertising. Here you can see a typical salutation that does nothing more than address the reader and support the belief they're reading a letter. It's from a piece of copy (by Stuart Goldsmith, I think) for a trading program called Secret Flag Trader from a chap called Guy Cohen:

> Tuesday 10.50am
>
> Dear Friend,
>
> Picture the scene...
>
> It's 1941 and the Nazi storm-
> troopers...

The addition of a time stamp is a nice touch, but the salutation itself is a simple "Dear Friend". Then it launches into a classic (and very successful) picture-based lead. Is the "Dear Friend" needed? Maybe not. But it doesn't jar too badly and it fulfils the traditional function of a salutation. I do think it could be stronger. I'll explain why in a moment. First, let's look at an example where I do think the salutation jars and makes itself redundant.

It's from a piece of copy for an American newsletter called *Retirement Millionaire*, published by an offshoot of The Agora called Stansberry & Associates Investment Research.

Now, the in-house copywriting team at Stansberry have produced some of the best financial direct-response copy of the modern age (they're behind the 'End of America' promotion I mentioned earlier). But here I think the traditional salutation is completely redundant:

> Dear Reader,
>
> Hello, my name is David.
>
> I've spent most of my life on...

See what I mean? The formal "Dear Reader" salutation is immediately followed by a more informal salutation of "Hello, my name is David". After reading the formal salutation, you almost have to reset and start the copy again. In such cases, the traditional salutation can be dropped completely.

Are you being impersonal by mistake?

Here's the problem: the traditional "Dear Reader" is pretty impersonal. It doesn't separate me – as a reader – from anyone else. The author of the copy could be addressing me, or they could be addressing the backgammon-playing crackpot who lives across the road. To better engage your reader, you need to be more specific. By the time you come to write your copy, chances are you've done a ton of research on who your target reader is. Scratch that. You should have definitely done a ton of research on who your target reader is. If not, go back and do so before writing another word. Once you have identified who you're writing to, you should be in a much better position to get a bit more specific.

Obviously, you don't want to drill down too deeply as you run the risk of alienating people. But something like this is ideal:

> Dear fellow photographer,
>
> **Start shooting like a pro**

This is from a piece of copy for a photography product written by my friend and fellow copywriter, Gerald Woodgate. He knows his stuff and here you can see he's tailored the salutation to "Dear fellow photographer". Personally I don't think it needs the "Dear". Just "Fellow photographer" feels smoother. But in a piece of copy written by a photographer to another photographer, this is excellent. If I were a keen photographer reading this, I'd immediately be more engaged and feel like it was addressing me directly. I think the 'Fellow X' salutation is one that can easily be applied to almost any piece of copy. You should try it. But it's not the only option.

Experiment with your salutations

I worked with a copywriter who wrote a letter for an educational forex product aimed at traders in financial markets who aren't having much success. (Don't worry if you haven't the foggiest what forex actually is – that's not what this is about.) The 'Fellow X' salutation could be deployed here: "Fellow trader" or even "Fellow forex trader", to be more specific. However, because the writer had done a lot of research and decided to aim at a specific type of forex trader, another option presented itself: we'll call it the 'Adjective X' salutation.

You see, instead of just addressing the reader by defining their niche, you can actually tap into their emotional state too. For example, you could begin: "Frustrated forex trader". As a forex trader I know the letter is addressing me, but now I know the author understands something about how I feel too. I feel a lot more engaged – I want to hear what this guy has to say.

Indeed, we all know the value of emotion in copywriting and adding even a slither more of it in your copy will undoubtedly add value. Whether you go this far is up to you, but I hope you can see now that there is a lot more to a simple salutation than you might have first thought. And of course, if you've seen a salutation that doesn't fall into the 'Fellow X' or 'Adjective X' category, test it. Heck, you might invent a whole new salutation technique yourself.

Top Tip

When you come to write any piece of copy, make sure you actually type out the salutation in your draft and always finish your copy by signing it off, even if it won't ultimately have your name at the end. This helps to remind you that your copy will be read by a real person. Even a basic salutation such as 'Dear Reader' helps remind you to keep things human. Hidden away behind a laptop screen, buried deep in all your research, it's so easy to get lost in your own head and forget who you're writing to.

Chapter Twelve
The Importance of Narrative

> *"We tell ourselves stories in order to live."*
>
> — *Joan Didion*

In our heads, we're all great storytellers

Years ago I had a series of meetings with one of those chaps who get all touchy-feely about what you really want to achieve in life and whether you're really doing what you want to do. You know the type. Speaks really slowly. Says "Sure, man, I get it," far too often. And has a weird inclination at the end of every sentence to say, "…or maybe you're the paranoid one?" and then nod in an overly deliberate way.

Most people react badly to these types. "What do you know about my problems, jerk… shove your faux-psychology up where it don't shine. I'm in complete control and I am meaning to be this stressed… so screw you and your Buddhist nonsense." Or maybe something slightly less angry. As far as I saw it, this particular guy was actually pretty smart and he didn't seem too touchy-feely. He wanted to offer practical advice and was self-aware enough to avoid the clichés of the trade.

Over the few sessions I had with him, I picked up a few interesting ideas that actually helped with my copywriting. Of course, that wasn't what I was supposed to get from the sessions, but it was a welcome bonus. One of the most interesting ideas that stuck in my mind was his skit on how small misunderstandings can spiral out of control when you don't communicate.

I'm really interested in communication and think most problems in the world – let alone in copy – are caused by a lack of it. Us humans were given the great power of being able to talk to each other in incredibly specific ways – yet we so often choose to mumble our way into unnecessary arguments and conflicts.

This self-help dude describes a situation where you're running late at work. It's completely innocent; you're just stuck in a meeting or whatever. And because you think it's 'nothing', you don't communicate to your partner. You figure the meeting will be over soon and they won't worry too much if you're a bit late. Fine. But the meeting goes on 30 minutes more and because you figured it was OK to begin with... you've still not told your other half. It'll be done soon. It's, er, OK. And sure, at home, you're partner is thinking... that's weird, they're normally home by now... must be held up at the office. Still, all fine. For now. But the boss still won't quit it and that suck-up member of staff you all hate keeps asking questions for no reason.

Meanwhile, it's an hour at home now and you're partner is really starting to think something is wrong... they wonder if you're in the pub drinking... they wonder if you're having an affair... they wonder if you've had an accident on the way home. You're still just sat in a meeting sneering at why Jimmy in customer services still doesn't get it... and why your boss won't just tell him to 'do one'. But back at home, as far as your partner is concerned... you're dead. They figure you wouldn't have not told them if you were having a drink... you're butt ugly so you can't be having an affair... so you simply must have veered off the motorway and be laid at this very moment in a ditch with the steering wheel jammed into your throat. Your partner is worrying about life insurance... funeral arrangements... how soon it will be before it's socially acceptable for them 'to see other people'... "OH GOD, WHAT WILL I TELL THE KIDS," they wonder?

You finally get out the meeting to find 30 missed calls from various members of your family, answering machine messages lamenting your death and a confused life insurance salesman asking you to call urgently. The point of the exercise was to show how – even in a completely innocent situation – a lack of communication could lead to a huge misunderstanding. But, ever on the lookout for copywriting insight, I saw something else too.

It's human nature to tell stories

The way the misunderstanding escalates so easily rang true to me. And I'm sure you can imagine how such an escalation could easily develop between you and your own partner in similar circumstances. What's interesting is that it reminds us of a fact of human nature. We are great at telling ourselves stories. And more than that. We are very good at filling in blanks with magnificent flights of fancy. When it comes to writing copy, we so often try to present complete pictures to readers. And we make assumptions that our beautifully painted pictures will look the same in their minds as they do in ours. But how realistic is that?

Take a simple income forecast...

I say you could make an extra £20,000 over the year and I think you will agree that's a pretty good extra income. And sure, if your income is £20,000 at the moment, you probably will think that's great. You're doubling your income. But if you already make £200,000, an extra £20,000 isn't going to seem quite as impressive. But if I say you could make thousands of pounds a month in extra income. How much do you imagine that could be? Obviously it now depends on your current income. If you earn £20k, you'll probably imagine one or two extra thousand a month... and you'd be happy with that. If you earn £200k, you'll probably think about an extra £10 or £20k a month... and you'd be happy with that. See what I mean?

A seasoned copywriter reading this will be thinking that I appear to be recommending being vague in copy, which is akin to recommending a vegan eat steak tartar. Don't worry: I've not gone mad. Specificity is STILL the rule of thumb. BUT there are moments when you can benefit from letting the reader do the painting.

Let your reader imagine how big the opportunity could be – don't let your income put a limit on their potential income. Let your reader picture their perfect life – don't let your imagination put a limit on their imagination. And let your reader think about what they have at risk – don't let your fears put a limit on theirs. Sometimes, when it comes to considering the narrative elements in your copy, you can save yourself some work and let the reader tell their own story.

I was like...

I'm sure you've noticed how young people these days seem to say 'like' incredibly often. I've seen a ton of comedians point out this strange little inflection, calling it the unfinished simile.

Probably you remember that word – simile – from some far away English language class, right? Basically, a simile is a figure of speech comparing two things, often introduced with the word 'like' or 'as'. You know the score:

My headache is like a crash of rhinos.

That mangy cat looks like Donald Trump's hair.

I'm as hungry as a horse.

That kind of thing.

When it comes to writing promotions, advertisements, squeeze pages, e-letters, newsletters, guides, reports – any piece of writing where you're trying to communicate an idea – similes can help you enormously.

Harness the power of similes

You can use short sharp similes to intensify an idea. Friend and expert copywriter James Woodburn did this well in one of his pieces, comparing impending financial disasters to time bombs. And on the threat of hyperinflation, he wrote: "...it'll be like going 15 rounds in a bare-knuckle fight with Mike Tyson."

Not only can a good simile intensify an idea, it can also help to get a complicated idea across. Esoteric economic theories can be hard to explain, but you know straight off that a time bomb going off in your face or Mike Tyson slapping you about is not a good thing. The simile creates an association that enables the reader to much better understand the implications of the difficult economic theory.

Another good example of explaining a difficult idea with simile can be seen in a piece of copy I wrote many years ago. This use of simile tackles a problem nearly every sports tipping service faces. Have a read and see how it's handled here:

"Some Fridays, now and again, we might hit on a loss. It's just the nature of things.

No matter how much you perfect something and apply the most specific analysis… sometimes things just don't go how they should.

It's like cricket.

You see, Shane Warne was one of the best bowlers ever…

In an ideal world he'd throw the perfect ball every time. He would have always hit the ground where he'll get the most spin. That's how he got the batsman out.

But even Shane Warne wasn't perfect.

Of course, most of the time he'd throw the ball good. Get the result he was after. That's like when we hit our regular Friday and lock-in easy £64s, £32s and £41s.

Sometimes though, he'd throw a big full toss…

They really get the batsman scared. They're exhilarating. Those extreme balls are like those big profits we could pull in – the £81os. We won't get them all the time but now and again we secure them and it's a super Friday.

But then now and again, Warne would throw some 'short' balls…

They aren't ideal as it gives the batsman a great chance to whack the ball for six. And that's just like the times when we'll pick up an annoying loss.

It's frustrating but we know that it's only an anomaly and just like Shane Warne, the next few balls will be right on target, get the batsman out and we win overall.

That's what we're interested in, what happens overall. And last year, if you had followed each of my simple Friday instructions while I was still testing and checking out the system, you would have made a total of £2,400.

Remember, that's completely tax-free. Every single pound of profit you collect is yours to keep and spend however you wish. The money-grabbing government can't touch any of it."

This takes the simile all the way, really expanding on the idea. By using this extended simile, the reader is able to see the bigger picture. Of course, even the best bowler misses the mark sometimes, just like the best tipping service does. But overall he's still the best bowler.

Discovering a good simile is all about playing about with different ideas, but there's one important thing you must remember…

Universally understood

You need to make sure the simile is universal.

Time bombs. Mike Tyson. Cricket and Shane Warne. I'd say they're all universal. That's why they work. If James had used Henry Armstrong, people would think, who? He's a boxer too – and 15 rounds with him would have hurt – but he isn't universally known. So, make sure what you're comparing your original idea to is very well known.

Finally, for fun, my favourite simile. It's from *Blackadder*:

Baldrick: I have a very, very, very cunning plan.

Blackadder: Is it as cunning as a fox what used to be Professor of Cunning at Oxford University but has moved on, and is now working for the UN at the High Commission of International Cunning Planning?

Now that's a simile!

Top Tip

Before I became a direct-response copywriter, I think I'd only read two books written in the second person: *If On A Winter's Night A Traveller*, by Italo Calvino and *Bright Lights, Big City* by Jay McInerney. It was considered weird to write anything in the second person. But in the world of direct-response copywriting, writing in the second person is something I'd encourage you to do as often as possible. Wherever you can in your copy, you should change 'I' to 'you' and rejig the phrasing of the sentence so that it still makes sense. Do so and your copy will be much stronger and much more engaging for the person reading it.

That strange but effective second person viewpoint brings, you, the reader, into the writing. It can help make you, the reader, the hero of the piece. Even when it feels a bit weird – and when the dormant English teacher and grammar stalwart in you starts screaming because you've weirdly mixed up viewpoints in the same paragraph – do your best to ignore the voice in your head and go with what's *engagingly* good, not necessarily what's *grammatically* right.

Chapter Thirteen
The Paradox of Testimonials

"I knew him well."

— **Misquote from Shakespeare's Hamlet**

An industry based on testimonials

For months, an ex-partner of mine couldn't sit. In fact, she could hardly walk. And at the lowest point, it seemed like the problem would never go away. Physical therapists advised exercises, strapped tape across her bum and prescribed painkillers to mask the discomfort. Still, nothing improved. Eventually an MRI scan was ordered. The cause of the problem was discovered: a prolapse in the L4/L5 lumber region. To you and me: a slipped disc. It was bad. In layman's terms, the shock-absorber thing that sits between the little bony bits of your spine was protruding back and to the left. And like some mysterious shooter on the grassy knoll, the true cause was unknown. We just knew it had happened and it wasn't good. The next stage was drugs – lots of them. For weeks this girl laid in bed whilst nerve-slowing narcotics attempted to ease the pain. But it soon became clear that this wasn't working either.

From surgeon to pain-specialist to physical therapist, we searched for someone who could offer a solution to the problem. Each offered their ideas and in each case, it seemed to work for a while. But sooner or later we hit a problem, and soon after that point the answers always dried up. When it comes to back problems, I've come to realise that everyone has their own story. You probably have one. If you don't, you will at some point. It's just a matter of time. In fact, it's become clear to me that because no one really knows what's right or wrong when it comes to the spine, it's an industry based almost entirely on testimonials.

A simple folder of evidence

As this girl struggled on, taxi drivers would notice it was difficult getting into the car and advise garlic tablets to ease the joints, because they knew a guy who had the same problem. Waiters would see her standing between courses to relieve some of the pressure and advise a certain type of pillow because their wife had the same problem. Or a gym instructor would see her wriggling on a floor to build her core muscles and advise a different exercise because – guess what – they knew this woman who had the same problem. We'd hear testimonial after testimonial and in each case we couldn't help but wonder if the solution being shared this time would be the one to help solve the problem. That's the pull with testimonials – if it worked for them, why can't it work for me?

Eventually, one testimonial led us to a chiropractic physician in Cheam – a little town in Surrey just outside London. We went along to hear the spiel. Whilst waiting for our consultation, we were shown what amounted to a video sales letter. It seemed strange, but effective. Then, as we continued to wait, we picked up a folder which lay on the coffee table. In this folder was testimonial after testimonial. On the left hand-side of the page you could read a typed printout of the letter, whilst the original handwritten version could be read on the right. Interesting, I thought.

As we read through the folder we found letters from old women, young children and middle-aged men – all describing symptoms similar to hers and then explaining how the technique that the physician practices had helped to solve the problem. The folder was incredibly convincing. Before we'd even sat down for the consultation we had already been instilled with a sense of hope, a feeling that this could well be the right solution for her too.

Later that day, as we walked around Cheam Park, giving the whole thing some thought, this girl kept coming back to those testimonials that we'd read in the folder before the consultation itself. They had formed a platform of both trust and hope. Trust that after so many people had advised her badly, this physician was proven. And hope that people had been in this same position and had found the solution here.

I can't imagine her back will ever be 100% – it's just one of those things that happens and stays with you forever – but after she opted to work with the chiropractic physician in Cheam, she saw a significant reduction in pain and a huge improvement in her mobility.

Whether the testimonials we read in the folder were genuine or not and whether the consultation alone would have convinced us that she offered the right solution, I don't know. The point is those testimonials were there and they provided a strong and convincing basis to the consolation that followed.

Testimonials are powerful, then. But do people read them in copy? No, not all the time.

Generally, people don't read testimonials

Here's the deal. I'm going to say some things here that might break with copywriting tradition. But if you take on board what I'm saying, your understanding of how copy works will become much, much stronger. It is not the content of testimonials that people are interested in – they are only interested in the presence of testimonials. Of course, the content must relate to what you are selling, but aside from that, more often than not, it's not important what a testimonial actually says – it's just the fact that someone is saying it.

You're wrong, Glenn, people do read testimonials and copy performs better when they're included.

Yes. Copy does often perform better when testimonials are included. But no, people do not read them. I am right. And I can prove it. In fact, let me just explain why it is naïve to think that people are reading all your testimonials all the time.

A piece of copy written by a junior copywriter was not performing as well as I expected it to. To help highlight what was wrong with the copy, I used a new piece of software one of my tech friends had come across – heat mapping – which recorded how much attention readers gave to each section of the copy. The results were very interesting. I noted that hardly any attention was given to the testimonials. Readers were attentive to the copy preceding the testimonials, but when they reached the testimonial copy, the reader quickly scrolled past. Their attention was only captured again a little later. I reduced the space given to the testimonials and saw conversion increase by 2%. This was an interesting discovery, but there was more testing to be done. I was not ready to declare the testimonial redundant – deep down I knew they were conversion boosters. But at the same time, I knew there was a better way to handle them.

The copy for a new forex advisory service I had helped create was working well. As the service itself developed, the editor requested testimonials and they came flooding in. I knew they represented an opportunity to add further proof to the current control copy in the hope of increasing conversion. But at the same time, because of the previous tests I'd done using the heat mapping software, I knew readers were scanning over the testimonial sections of the promotion. I realised that the way testimonials have been used in promotional material in the past has stunted the power of good testimonials to the point now where it is not the content of testimonials that people are interested in – they are only interested in their presence.

When testimonials are included in copy they have the potential to increase response – because people see that other people are reporting positively about the product – but if you only list them one after the other, people will soon tire and begin to scan over them.

A better way to use testimonials

To encourage people to spend more time actually reading testimonials, as with any piece of copy, you should take the time to walk the reader through what's written. If you just plonk a large section of text on the page, it's probably going to look a bit daunting. As many testimonials aren't written by trained writers, the details that you'll want to pull out may be hidden. This is why I suggest you do three things to make sure you get the most out of the testimonials you do use.

First, you should condense the copy where you can. Of course, you cannot change the intention of the testimonial, nor can you add to it (unless you are in a position to enter into a dialogue with the writer of the testimonial and seek permission to adjust it). I merely suggest that you cut any copy from the testimonial that slows it down or doesn't promote the copy. For example, if the testimonial were to read:

> "Fine work, Glenn. I read your book the other day when I was on the bus and there was a guy who was playing his music loudly and very nearly put me off reading. But I thought your book was very good and I would recommend it to all of my friends. I hope you are well and look forward to hearing more about your dog."

Sure, such feedback would be lovely. But if you were to use it in a piece of copy, it is too long and filled with extraneous detail. Without changing the intent of the testimonial, you could easily reduce it to:

> "Fine work... your book was very good and I would recommend it to all my friends."

Here you've pulled out the key detail, the copy is much more concise and the message comes across loud and clear. If you're able to reduce your testimonials down like this, great. But if you're unable to omit details without changing the overall intent of the testimonial, there is second thing you can do to better handle them.

As I pointed out before, the problem lies in that people tend to scan over testimonials without considering the detail. The reader is more concerned with the narrative you've developed in your main copy. The solution? Work elements of your testimonials into the main copy. Rather than just shoehorning an entire paragraph into the copy as is traditionally done, pull out the key phrases and write them into your main copy. For example:

"When you get your hands on a copy of my book, you'll see for yourself why one reader says he'd 'recommend it to all my friends.'"

As part of the main copy, this smaller quote still has the effect of being a testimonial from a third party and it gets the message across in a focused way.

Top Tip

Don't shy away from negative testimonials. Embrace them and tackle them head on. Providing the product or service you're writing copy for is good and you can stand behind it, you can use negative testimonials in a positive way. Address the concerns they raise and provide counter arguments or explanations as to why the customer may have not had a good experience. When done successfully, overcoming objections this way can be extremely powerful and compelling.

Chapter Fourteen
Making An Offer

"Make him an offer he can't refuse."
— **Marlon Brando in The Godfather**

Forget your fancy ideas, they're nothing without value

The local shop in my village has finally figured out the perfect marriage of impulse purchase and value. There I am – waiting for the assistant to pack my stuff and ring it through the register – and I notice them. Four Kit Kats for £1. I know I shouldn't. But four... FOUR... for just £1. That's damn good value. Especially when you look across the counter and realise that one Kit Kat alone costs nearly 70p these days. You'd be dumb not to buy four for just £1.

What's this have to do with direct-response copywriting? I think we sometimes tend to get a little too philosophical about ideas and forget that behind all successful direct-response copy, there's usually a really good offer. And that offer is usually dressed up as what I'd call a *value proposition*. What do I mean by that? Let's take a look.

Ideas need offers

You are never going to write a truly breakthrough, business-changing piece of copy without a great idea. A good offer alone will help the business tick over and it might even be seen as a clever idea in itself. Take something like *The Economist* offering 12 issues for £12. It's kind of an idea in itself. Really it's just a good offer and has probably done their business well. But it won't ever transform the business, not fundamentally. Only a truly great idea can do that. But a truly great idea still needs a good offer behind it to really work. Even with the best idea ever, you're never going to get the click without offering your reader a strong value proposition.

Don't forget: the whole concept of direct-response copy is to get a *direct-response* from the reader. And what better way to do that than to offer them value: I'll give you this, if you give me that.

What do I mean by value? Four Kit Kats for £1 is good value because I can measure it against my own perception of what a Kit Kat costs. I have a perceived cost for a Kit Kat of around 70p. Note that it's irrelevant how much Kit Kats actually cost – it's what I think they cost that's important. If you offer me four for £1, I can make a quick assessment and figure, sure, that's good value. I'm in.

That's the same process you need to recreate when it comes to offering a value proposition in your copy. You need to make an offer that appears to provide value when measured against your reader's perception of the cost of what you're selling. And it needs to be obvious. X is worth Y, but I'm only paying Z. Great, I'm in. Sometimes that'll be easy. If you're selling something tangible, such as a book or a guide, and your offer is for less than the cost of the item, it should obviously be good value. You won't need to do too much extra here (though ideally you still should).

But often you'll be selling something that's less tangible than Kit Kats, like a service of some description; something with a less obvious perceived cost. This makes it a little harder because your reader has nothing to measure the cost against. Their perceived value of your product or service might be significantly different to what you value it at. What do you do in this instance? The answer is simple. But it might also need you to go back to the client to improve their offering. Here's why...

Emotional decisions need logical reasoning

If you've got a good idea and your copy has emotionally connected with the reader then they will be ready to buy. They're engaged. They're excited. They're going to tell the world about this.

Ah, but there's the problem. They're going to need to justify the purchase to someone. It might be their partner, their family, or their team at work. Maybe it's just themselves. Whoever it is, before you can close the sale, you're going to need to help your reader justify the sale to them. You see right now, as you ask for £100 to subscribe to your service, the reader is thinking: is this worth £100? What will my partner say? What have I actually got to show for this idea I've been sold on? Argh! I'm losing faith in this whole venture. And what do you mean I can get my money back? Why would I need to get my money back?

Of course, earlier in the copy you should have been loading up your argument with proof of all different kinds, which will go a long way to helping your reader justify the purchase. But to close the sale, in addition to the proof you've given them, you should offer them obvious value above and beyond their perceived cost of the product or service you're selling.

This could come in the form of:

- A gift related to the product or service that adds some tangible value – you can speak to your client and ask them what material they have that you could pitch as an additional gift.

- A voucher or credit redeemable on something else – a great copywriter in the US called Joe Schriefer literally offered people a blank cheque, which is perhaps the best example I've ever seen of this.

As you can see, there are many ways to add value to your offer – and if possible, I would recommend doing them all at the same time. Seriously. The more you can add to go above and beyond their perceived cost of your product or service, the more effective your offer will be.

The lesson here is simple: Once you've done all the work finding your idea, engaging the reader and proving to them why your idea is so cool, don't stop there. All good direct-response copy needs a good offer to close the deal. You need to stop, reset your thinking and ask how you can provide value to the reader that is in excess of their perceived cost of the product or service you're selling. Do that and you'll see the sales flying in.

Your offer should be relevant to the product

Where did the 30-day trial come from? Seriously – if you know, please write and tell me. If you've written copy for online products or services, no doubt you know the 30-day trial well. Or maybe, if you've written for a product or service that's being sold on Clickbank or some other joint venture website, you've probably come across its older brother: the 60-day trial. To be honest, I'm fed up of both.

Sure, they work. They're proven offers that have incentivised people to buy Product X or try Service Y. But still: I just think we can do better. As copywriters, I feel it's our duty to understand what motivates people to buy and when we see opportunities to better motivate people, we should tackle them. And so here's my problem…

I feel like trial periods in copywriting have become stale. It's like when you join a new company and ask: "Why do we do this obviously inefficient thing like this?" And the only answer you get is: "Because that's how we've always done it." That, to me, is the reason the vast majority of copy is written to include a 30-day trial period. Do you agree? Or rather, are you open to the idea that there might be a better way to deal with trial offers? I hope so. Indeed, assuming you're with me here, let's actually look at why we offer trial periods at all in copy. There are actually a few reasons.

First, it's so that people have the opportunity to try something that is ultimately speculative with the assurance that – if it doesn't work out as promised – you can get your money back. I think I remember some old-school ad-man like Drayton Bird writing that it was washing machines that started this – but I may have made that up.

Second, everyone else does it. This is a reason; don't forget it. It's the same reason so many people offer free delivery on stuff. Once upon a time, free delivery wasn't a given like it is today. But slowly the market has changed and now you simply have to offer it to compete. That's how it is with trial periods too. You look weird if you don't offer one.

Finally, it takes the risk out of the buying decision. When someone is contemplating a product or service, the decision to purchase is made much easier if they know they can change their mind in a month's time.

We can all accept that there is reason enough to include a trial period in your copy. The problem I have is not with the principle; it's the execution.

I propose that there is no reason for a trial period to be limited to the arbitrary ranges of 30 or 60 days.

A trial period should allow a potential customer to trial said product or service for such a time that they can establish if said product or service actually delivers on the promises made elsewhere in the copy. Fair enough, right? And so in accepting this fact we must look again at the product or service we're writing copy for and ask: how long would a customer really need to use this to be able to confirm the promises made are achievable?

By natural extension we can suggest that a product that requires 16 days to mature, needs a 16-day trial period. While a service that promises X within a year, *really* requires a trial period of the same. Of course, the business minds amongst us will question the sense in risking such an extensive period in which you could hand back money on a service, but surely... if said business is not committed to its services delivering, there are bigger worries.

What I'm really suggesting here is that we think a little more about the product or service itself and ask if there's a way we can play it that a three-week trial period might actually be more appropriate to the copy we're writing, than the arbitrary 30-day offer.

Sure, 21 days is actually less than 30 days and is technically a worse guarantee period. But if the promise in your copy is that the reader will have completed X in 21 or days' time or made Y within three weeks, then it's going to seem more convincing if your trial period gives that reader the exact time they need to achieve the aim. Indeed what's the alternative? You've got three weeks and then another nine days because it might not work and that gives you a bit longer.

You hopefully see what I'm saying. It's not a big thing. It's just something that many overlook. Yet at the same time, it's such an easy thing to fix. Next time you come to writing an offer that includes a typical and essentially arbitrary trial period of 30 or 60 days, stop. Think about it and question if there isn't a way to make your trial period more apt.

Make sure you're not misusing this word

As well as worrying about sentence structure over breakfast, I also worry about one particular word used in copy. It's damaging. It's disingenuous. And for me it's a sign that you've hired a lazy (or even bad) copywriter. Or worse, your product or service is weak. And all this thanks to the misuse of one simple word! Don't worry though; it's a simple fix.

Whether you write sales copy yourself, or if you need to review others' copy for your own business, being able to spot the misuse of this word will significantly increase how effective that copy is.

What's the word that's so often misused? The word that will stunt your sales? As you've probably guessed, it's "unique".

But that's one of the Four Us! A good piece of sales copy should be useful, ultra-specific, urgent and... unique.

Indeed, it should. You're exactly right. But you should not just state that something is unique. The key is to state why it is unique. My hair is pretty unique. I doubt there's another person out there who's wearing the exact same number of strands that are all the exact same length as mine and are all going off in the exact same directions. Yes, my hair is unique. But that doesn't necessarily mean it's good. In fact, it's quite bad. But what the stylists at Toni & Guy might think of my hairstyle is irrelevant. The important thing is that you realise that simply stating something is unique is not enough.

Good copywriting must go deeper. If I was trying to say why you should like my hair, I might say it's quite thick. It's medium brown. There's an increasing amount of grey. When I was a kid I could use it to cover up my ears, which used to stick out a bit. Nowadays, if it gets too long it starts getting a bit curly. You see, by digging a little deeper behind why something is unique, you start to pull out interesting details.

Let's apply that theory to a product or service.

Say you're hired to write copy for a firm that books event spaces for special occasions. They want you to write some copy for their new brochure that encourages businesses to book their special events through them. They tell you they're the industry leader and they are really good at booking event spaces. They assume that will be enough information. Once you've calmed down, you ask the all important question…

Why is it unique?

Aha!

The problem is that many companies believe so inherently in their own business that they forget the reason why other people would find their business interesting. They forget that the competition often believe the exact same about their business. Just being 'good' is not enough. You've got to dig deeper. In asking what makes the product or service unique, you will uncover more saleable details. It might be that the company you're writing for is the only company who provides a complete solution to your event booking, not just dealing with the venue. This could give your copy that all important edge.

If those interesting details are missing from your sales copy, if it just says "XYZ is unique", you need to go back to the product or service and dig deeper. Keep digging until you uncover that special detail that makes the product or service stand out and then use that detail to strengthen your sales message. If you've got a good product or service, a product or service that you believe in, the special details that do make it unique will soon reveal themselves. You just need to tease them out.

Top Tip

Present the price of what you're selling in a way that makes it seem more palatable. £100 might seem like a lot to spend on an e-book reader, for example. But if you break it down to be less than 30p a day to read all the books you'll ever need, it can seem much better value. Alternatively, look to transfer the cost to something the customer already recognises and takes for granted. Spending £1,000 for a year of access to expert financial advice might sound expensive, but when you consider it's less than you'd spend on a cup of coffee each day, it seems a much more reasonable investment.

Chapter Fifteen
If In Doubt, Cut It Out

> *"I know you love this bit, and it's really nicely written.*
> *But you know you need to delete it."*
>
> **— John Forde, reviewing a piece of my copy**

Avoiding waffle

Recently, I went out for a drink with some of the best copywriters in the UK. We spent most of the evening talking about sales writing and what made a piece of copy successful. And to be perfectly honest, the answer is a bit elusive. No one really knows exactly what makes one piece of writing successful and another not. It's just a case of testing pieces against each other, changing different elements to see what works and what doesn't. But when it comes to getting a click, you can learn a lot by learning what you shouldn't do.

In this chapter, I'm going to tackle a range of different techniques you can use to keep your copy succinct, crisp and free of waffle.

I don't want to have to use this gun

Imagine for a moment you're living a roguish life as a bank robber in the Wild West. You drift from ramshackle town to ramshackle town sticking up the local bank and then drifting on. You're damn good at it too. Just yesterday you moseyed on in, stuck your gun in the bank teller's face and said your usual "This is a stick-up" line. The teller knew the score straightaway and handed over the bag of swag. You moseyed on out. But you have a secret past…

You weren't always that good. You used to get yourself in some real scrapes, almost getting caught by the sheriff every time you tried a stick-up.

What changed?

Back then, you'd mosey on in to the bank and it would go something like this: "I am known as the Wild Man of Wyoming. I've travelled for many days and I have arrived upon your town. I have entered your bank and intend to leave with the contents of your safe. You can see here I have a gun and I will use it if required. I don't want to have to use this gun so please take this empty bag and fill it with the contents of the safe I mentioned before. While you do that I will…"

Already someone has sneaked out of the bank and has run to the sheriff's office. You see the problem with your old approach was that you said too much. Your new line – "This is a stick-up" – says everything your previous approach did, but it does it in just four words.

Good copywriting is the same. So many people make the mistake of waffling. Years of testing has proved that long copy works well – long letters and adverts that take the time to argue and prove the case for a product or service are effective. But too many people confuse writing a lot with saying a lot.

Just because you write a lot, doesn't mean you're saying anything more than if you wrote less. Take Hemingway's famous and often cited six word story: "For sale: baby shoes, never worn." Just six words, but it says so much more.

How do you avoid waffling and make sure you're saying what you need to say as effectively as you can? Good news is, it's not difficult. You've just got to be strict with yourself.

Start out as normal. Write as much as you want. Waffle on. But then when you're through waffling, forget about it. Walk away. Leave it a few hours, even a day, and then go back to what you've written. Keep in mind the point you're trying to make and re-read the piece. Anything that doesn't refer to your original point in some way, get rid. As I say, be strict and if in doubt, take Hemingway's advice and cut it out.

What you'll be left with is a much more effective piece of writing that is easier and more enjoyable to read. By practising this technique you'll start to write less and less waffle first time round and you'll see that your first draft will become much tighter and require less editing.

The three-strike process for writing better copy

This is a little technique you can use to ensure that your writing is always direct and to the point. This might seem quite clinical and drastic, but it does work. Read through your piece of writing and after each paragraph ask yourself, "So what?" If you can answer that question, or the next paragraph does so, then that's fine. But if not, consider that a strike. Read the next paragraph. Ask the question again. Is the reason for that paragraph explained? Is there a clear benefit? If so, good stuff. Reset your strike count and continue. If not, though, clock up another strike.

Read through your piece following this process. If you get to three strikes and a reason or benefit of continued reading is not obvious then stop. Work needs to be done. It's at this point that you run the risk of losing any potential reader. It's therefore incredibly important that you insert a benefit related to the product or service at this point, or in one of the three previous paragraphs. You need to make it a benefit that gives the reader a reason to continue reading the story.

For example, take a look at this section from a sales letter I wrote:

> "This guy's never set foot on a trading floor. The most he's ever won on the lottery is two lots of £10. His parents haven't got anything more than a regular couple in their 60s. And he's straight up, not a dodgy deal in sight."

So what? At this point there's no clear reason why you should read on. That's strike one. But let's carry on:

> "He's got a load of angles, different income streams, different systems. But he's adamant: the systems themselves are irrelevant."

So what? It's a little intriguing, but if we're clinical about it, there's no clear reason to read on. Strike two. We're in the waffle zone now. Let's move on cautiously:

> "This is key. Get it and seriously: you're already half way to a regular second income. You'll see how if you do what this man did, £1,960, £2,438, or even £3,828 a month is easily within reach."

Bingo: an explicit benefit and an obvious reason why the reader should read on. The strike count can be reset and you can continue assessing the rest of the piece.

As you write and review more copy, you'll get a more natural feel for when this danger point occurs and it won't always be necessary for you to go through this three-strike process. But it does help. And following it will increase the effectiveness of any piece of advertising.

Plus this technique can be used on any piece of sales writing, no matter its length. A three-line advert for example: if you're still saying "so what?" after the third line, you've got a problem. Or if you're writing a job application (a job application is just another piece of sales writing): if your potential employer is reading your application and asks "so what?" more than three times you can pretty much be sure you're not getting an interview.

Next time you need to sell anything with a piece of writing, try asking "so what?" and use the three-strike process to see how you can improve the piece.

How come these sentences are so short?

Now, it's time to be honest with me. Did you do the rote learning exercise that I detailed earlier in the book? I hope so. If you did, there are things you now know about direct-response copywriting that you probably don't even realise. I'll explain more in a minute.

First, I'm going to give you one quick minute to own up if you didn't write out the sales letter. If, for some reason, you didn't have a chance –

take a moment to do it now. Seriously, before you go any further, take half an hour to sit down and write out the copy. It will help you no end.

But what am I saying… of course you did it. You're focused. You're eager to achieve. And you know that following the steps I lay out for you in each chapter of this book will help you to learn a skill that will enable you to transform your business or career. So, let's crack on.

One of the first things you'll have noticed in copying out the sales letter would have been the shortness of the sentences and paragraphs. In fact, it's a bit like this entire book, right? Everything seems to be cut up. Short little blasts of text that are pretty easy to read. Sometimes, you might even think you're reading faster than you would normally.

You're right to spot it. It's intentional. It's the first lesson you've learned. Maybe without even realising it! But what a lesson: learning to write in this short, simple and straightforward way will help you massively. Obviously it comes with practice and there are numerous ways to proactively teach yourself to write in this style, but by far the best way to master this style is this…

Writing more clear and concise copy

This is a trick I teach any copywriter or editor I work with. It isn't difficult. It isn't time consuming. And it certainly isn't fancy. In fact, it's a very simple and purely technical change you make to your word processor each time you're writing copy. It's particularly effective for articles, blog posts, auto-responder copy and short adverts. It also returns great results for any copy that will be read on a mobile device. But anyway, before I explain how to set this trick up, let us briefly consider the philosophy behind it. I mean, I don't want to encourage a lazy generation of copywriters. I do this as standard now and so should you.

People have always complimented my copywriting style. They say it appeals to them. That it's clear and concise. But here's the thing. There's no reason why you can't write in the same way. The simple reason my writing is clear and concise – most of the time – is because I force myself to adapt it to the way we consume copy. Consider this: nearly

70% of subscribers read my AllGoodCopy.com email newsletter on a mobile phone. It follows that the screen on a mobile phone is relatively thin – you can't get much on a line. So, if your copy is 'thin' – if you restrict how much is on a line – it makes it easier to read.

But this is nothing new. Before mobile, people read their copy in email inboxes. They are thin too. Most of the window is taken up by functionality and online adverts. And before that? People read their copy in newspapers and magazines and the copy in those was… yup, you guessed it: thin. It was specifically designed to be printed in columns. Why? Because it meant there was less copy on one line, so it made it easier to read.

As I say, this is not a new idea. It's just that a lot of people seem to have forgotten about it. I haven't and nor should you. In fact, you should think about it regularly. Official figures vary, but somewhere between 55% and 75% of all email is now read on mobile. One report predicts that by end of 2018, 80% of people will read their email on a mobile device. That's huge. And when writing copy, it's something you must be aware of.

A really simple thing you can do to immediately improve your writing for mobile is to remember to keep your subject lines short. On mobile devices many subject lines run off the screen and can therefore make any cleverly crafted sentences meaningless. Aside from run-off, some mail applications now cut the middle of an email subject line and replace with an ellipsis. A crude example: "Really glad I don't hate this thing," could become "Really glad I… hate this thing." The meaning is completely changed. As a general rule of thumb, I would look to keep subject lines between 50–70 characters, which usually equates to around 10–15 words. Also, where possible, try to front load your subject lines so that if words do get chopped off at the end, the reader can still get the gist of the message from the start of the subject line.

The chances are that by the end of 2018, 80% of your copy could be read on a mobile device. Do you think people are going to scroll through long, dense paragraphs of copy? No chance. Just like with the subject lines, you need short, sharp sentences. You need paragraphs broken up by exclamations. You need copy that doesn't give someone thumb-ache. The good news is – thinking about these factors automatically results in your copy being more clear and concise. It just happens. Like magic.

But let me be clear: this isn't something you should only consider when writing copy delivered by email. Whether your copy is being read on the blog page of a company website, in the Sunday supplement of a national newspaper, or on the overhead panel of a London Underground train, you should always aim to make it short, snappy and as easy to read as possible. White space is a good friend of copy and you should make sure your words always have plenty of room to breathe.

Here's where we get to the technical trick I mentioned earlier…

The wonders of the modern day word processor

After all this preamble, you're hoping this is going to be the revelation of the decade, right? Well, er, jeez, I think I might need a lawyer.

Basically, all you need to do in Microsoft Word is set your margin to 13, change your font to Courier New and change the font size to 10. Ta-da! Hmmm. You're not satisfied. But you should be. Whether you realise it or not, I've just revealed a purely functional change to the way you write that will infinitely improve your ability to write copy. By limiting yourself in this way, you'll start to notice a number of things.

Firstly, there will be a lot more white space around what you write. As I say, white space is your friend: you want as much of it as possible. It means your copy will be much more appealing to the eye, be it on a laptop, a mobile phone or in print. Good copy should look like it's going to be an easy read.

Secondly, you'll notice that when you type over four lines of text, your paragraph will seem a little flabby. That's because it probably is. So, cut it down. This isn't a hard and fast rule, but it's pretty damn close. Only very rarely can you make the case for five or six lines of copy in this format. So, don't be afraid to break your paragraphs up with exclamations.

Like this.

Although try not make them as obvious or as laboured as that. They should enhance the copy by giving the reader a chance to breathe, whilst still being engaged in the flow of your copy.

Finally, when it comes to longer pieces of copy – a section of a book like this, for example – this format will give you a good indication of how long it is. You'll be able to see more objectively whether it needs breaking up with subheadings (roughly one per page of copy) or even dividing into separate parts (attention naturally wanes after more than three pages in this format). All in all, it's just a damn easy way to very quickly cheat your way to cleaner copy.

That said, when it comes to writing much longer copy, I do tend to use a different format, usually Arial, font size 14, set at a margin of 15. It has the same effect but is easier to work with on longer projects. For now, you should use this formatting technique for all your copy as it's perfect for anyone who's just starting out and it's good practice for writing in the clipped style that is a feature of successful copy.

Good fish and chips but a really bad advert

"The Very Best Fish and Chips... Around." So read the sign outside my old local pub. Sounds good, right? In fact, a while back I popped in for lunch – it was a nice piece of fish. But I didn't go in because of the sign. I only noticed that on my way home one night. When I did I sighed. What a terribly written sign. I'll tell you why and how you can make sure that whenever you're required to write a short advert for something you don't waste the opportunity like my local pub has.

I accept that "The Very Best Fish and Chips..." is a good start. It tells you about the product the pub is selling and it makes a good promise – these fish and chips are the very best. But with that pregnant pause, that ellipsis, it all falls apart and a massive opportunity is missed. With such a short advert you've got chance to do two things: the claim and the clincher.

Those two things are fairly self-explanatory. The claim needs to make a claim, one that grabs the reader's attention by identifying the thing on offer and making it stand out from the crowd. In a short advert like the pub sign, or a small banner ad, or a pay-per-click advert, the claim will usually be your first line. The clincher is your second line and needs to add something to your claim. The pub sign falls down because it takes away from the claim.

To begin with you're thinking, "These are the very best fish and chips." Great stuff. Can't wait. But when you read on you realise that they're only the best fish and chips "around". How far is "around"? Does it cover the next block? Just the street, or maybe just around that particular corner?

OK, I'm being a little pedantic here, but the fundamental point remains: by saying "around" you're making a concession. You're undermining your claim. And when you do that, you're losing your reader. You're losing your customer. What you need to do is clinch the deal.

For example: "The Very Best Fish and Chips… and a free pint", is much stronger. Why? Because the addition of "a free pint" is a great clincher: you're getting the very best fish and chips and a free pint. The deal's done, you've attracted a customer.

When it comes to writing a small two line advert – be it a sidebar, a banner, a pay-per-click ad, or a small sign – always make the most of the limited space by breaking it down to two lines: your claim and your clincher.

The use of ellipses in copy

I mentioned ellipses, those three dots that you'll often see used at the end of a sentence or linking one to another. In copy ellipses are ready money. People use them a lot. I use them myself and like many others I have been guilty of overusing them.

They're good for two reasons. Firstly, for creating flow. An ellipsis at the end of a paragraph helps to lead the reader onto the next paragraph as they expect something more. It works like this…

Hello again! You see the end of that previous paragraph flowed much easier into the next. But remember that it is an artificial flow. You should aim as often as possible to allow your paragraphs to flow into each other without the addition of an ellipsis.

The second way you can put ellipses to good use is as a pausing technique. When reading the example before of the flowing paragraphs, you might not even have noticed, but when faced with an ellipsis you pause your reading for a moment. It's this pause that lets you breathe and creates the flow I mentioned before, but you can also use this pause to surprise the reader and add power or emphasis to the following line.

The pub sign story above is a good example of how it works, but a bad example of how to do it. You pause on the '…' after the "very best fish and chips" bit, and then you're surprised by the "around". As we've seen though, the word "around" doesn't work as a clincher and doesn't make best use of the ellipsis pause.

Ideally you should use ellipses sparingly, as by doing so you enhance their effectiveness when you do use them. Keep an eye out for adverts and examples where the claim and clincher technique is used, or wherever you see ellipses put to good (or bad) use.

Top Tip

Have a couple of friends among your contacts who you can ask to review your writing. Your partner. Your friend from school. Your dad. Your grandma even. The key is you have a couple of people who you trust to be open with criticism and won't be offended by any disagreement you might have. The openness is essential. If you haven't got a copywriting peer group yet, you should try to cultivate one as quickly as possible, as it will make you a much more successful copywriter. No direct-response copy should be published unless it's had at least one other set of eyes on it.

Chapter Sixteen
Time Management Tips for Writing Copy

> *"Don't spend time beating on a wall, hoping to transform it into a door. "*
>
> **- Coco Chanel**

Your most important asset is time

Copywriting should be fun. It should be challenging too. But if you're finding it too challenging, it's wearing you down or it's taking up too much of your time, you're probably doing something wrong. So here I want to give you some tips on how to better manage your time when writing copy. Most of this comes from my own personal experience and is a reaction to how I tend to work personally. Needless to say, some of my ideas might not suit you 100%. But hopefully they might inspire you to invent your own approach. Indeed, here are five top tips to help you write more effectively in a lot less time…

1. Turn off, tune out

When you sit down to write, do just that. Write. Eliminate all other distractions. I've started with a real cliché here, but it is completely and utterly necessary. Why? Because the world is constantly getting better at creating distractions we don't even realise are distractions. Your phone. Your inbox. That email that needs answering right now, even though it's just a vague question about something happening next week. Your colleague across the room who keeps humming. The glint of the sun on the mirror over there. The food downstairs that needs eating. The 15th cup of tea you need to make before you finish this next bit.

I know you know why distractions waste time, so I'm not going to go into it too deep. But one thing I would recommend is making sure you tell anyone who might potentially distract you unwittingly that you are going to be dead to the world from moment X through period Y. Eventually people will get the point that you write at this time.

2. The reason there are so many Jeeves and Wooster stories

PG Wodehouse was a great writer. If you've not read any of his work, you really should – especially as a copywriter. Aside from being very funny, his writing is sharp. It's pacey. And it's not at all fussy (despite some of the characters being extremely so). His writing shares a lot of the key qualities of good copy. Most likely if you've read any Wodehouse, you'll have read some of his Jeeves and Wooster stories, about an idiot toff and his cynically smart butler. Indeed, there are loads of Jeeves and Wooster stories. But there are loads of Psmith stories too (another of his recurring characters). And there are loads of Blanding stories. And there are loads of... you get the point. The guy churned out a lot of copy over the years.

How? I think it has something to do with his approach to writing: he is reported to have fixed himself to a very strict daily routine whereby he would allocate a set amount of time to write each day in the morning. In his more youthful years he would rack up around 2,500 words between breakfast and lunch. But even in later life he still managed to commit 1,000 words to the page. Of course, it wasn't all good stuff. But by setting time aside each day, and just writing, he always came out of every session with something he could use. If you allocate at least some fixed time to your writing each day then you'll come away with something too.

3. Finish on a cliffhanger

I think I read somewhere that this idea is attributed to something Hemingway said about his writing. Hemingway suggested that each day, when coming to the end of your period of writing, you should finish halfway through a sentence or idea. We're literally talking halfway through the…

See what I did there. The idea is that if you're at a point in your writing where you're engaged and know how it's flowing, you should stop. You would think it would be an idea to continue apace if you know where you're going, but you'll probably only tire and fizzle out soon anyway and the next day you won't know where to go and could lose all of the day to burnout or a lack of inspiration.

But if you stop halfway through an idea on day one, you know for sure that on day two you're going to pick it up again just where you left of and push on again full of fresh steam. I do this a lot myself and it does help. One of the hardest things about writing is dealing with the blank page, wondering where to go next. But this cliffhanger approach, though seeming to be somewhat counterintuitive, is actually pretty useful. Try it.

4. Let the meat rest

Immediate reviewing of copy you have just written is sure to waste a ton of your time. Upon finishing a first draft, you're far too close to it to be able to do any effective editing. You're going to miss loads of stuff. You're going to be far too soft on yourself because you're tired. And you're going to spend twice as long achieving half as much as you would if you waited. Just like you should always let your meat rest for a while after it's cooked, you should let your copy rest too.

Go and do something else – preferably unrelated to copy. Whereas a nice gammon joint should be let to rest for about 15 minutes, copy should be left to rest for at least 24 hours, or at least overnight. When you return to the scene of the crime the next day, you'll do so with a fresh, critical eye and you'll do a much better review job.

5. The cooling off period

Just as you should give your copy a rest between reviews, you need to give yourself a rest between major projects. Not many people talk about this, and perhaps you've never experienced it yourself. But my sense is that you might just relate to it. You see, whenever I finish a major project, for a couple of days I'm a bit spaced out. If you've done your job properly, your head will be full of research about the product, your thoughts will be fizzled, and your ability to write a coherent sentence will probably be shot. To get straight back on the horse at this stage, so to speak, would be daft. Again, everything you do in this state of mind will take longer, be less effective and likely end up needing more work on it at a later date.

Rather than feel guilty about the fact you're frazzled and can't work as well, admit to it. Own it. And make it a positive. Be self-aware enough to understand that you waste everyone's time when you waste your own time. Instead, give yourself a rest. Take a day out of the system completely. Purge yourself of the product you were writing for. Purge yourself of the act of writing and thinking completely and do something else. Properly rested, you'll be able to attack the next project with total dedication and unwavering energy.

And there you have it: five things you can do to reduce the stress and strain of facing the blank page and make sure you're using your time as effectively as you can. When you next feel like you're procrastinating, or you've reached a point where the words don't seem to be coming, take a moment to check yourself, be self-aware and ask yourself if your time wouldn't be more effectively spent on something else other than copy.

Top Tip

When you send out a piece of copy and it doesn't work, before you throw it away and write off all the time you spent on it... stop and think. You see, despite the seeming failure, you now have something black and white on your hands. You know something in that copy definitely does not work. You can overthink things at this stage, but the problem is most often one of three things:

1. People just aren't interested in the idea.

2. It's the wrong time for the idea.

3. People don't understand the idea.

In the first two instances, there's not a lot you can do. If people aren't interested in the idea, you'll waste a lot of time trying to tweak something that is fundamentally broken. You need to accept that a bad idea got through your radar and see it as a learning exercise to be more disciplined before you write up an idea. If it's not the right time for an idea, again, you can't change the market or try to convince it the time is right... so don't bother. Put your copy to the side and make a note to revisit it if you see the market sentiment changing.

In the third instance, where people don't understand the idea, you can try a new headline that overtly and more explicitly expresses the idea. If you see any increase in conversion here, you have a clue that it is a case of people not getting it, and you can now spend some more time rewriting your idea so people do.

Chapter Seventeen
Sell, or Share?

"If it doesn't sell, it isn't creative."

— *David Ogilvy*

Questioning David Ogilvy

"Sell, or else," pronounced legendary ad man, David Ogilvy. And, ever since, this unflinching commandment has been passed down from copywriter to copywriter. It's the great leveller; the simple reminder that whatever the media, your aim remains the same: you sell, my friend, you sell if it's the last thing you do. But is it the *right* aim? Or rather, is it the right *message*? Is the perceived wisdom of *a sale above all else* the idea we still want to convey to our budding salespeople? Is it a legacy we want to help sustain?

I've thought a lot about this. It's an issue that's been skirting around me for a while: a tangential discussion here, an email thread there. I guess I'll go through the thoughts and you can consider them with me. Perhaps even share yours on the subject too. I hope you do. But before I begin, I should own up.

For many, many years I've been a great believer in the wisdom of Ogilvy. I've preached his gospel with great gusto. I still do: one of the first books my trainee writers are told to read is *Ogilvy on Advertising*. So, of course I'm not suggesting he's run his course completely – that would be madness. Still, to paraphrase the great American novelist Saul Bellow: there's no point in reading something unless it bites you. And in that spirit, I'll come out and damn well say it:

David Ogilvy is wrong.

Yes. I want to challenge the late, great Ogilvy and suggest that today, as a business, you must actually "share, or else." Ugh. Really? Is that the best alternative? A statement so laced in social media sentiment it's enough to make you puke. Surely not! Honestly I'm not sure myself and I'm open to suggestions. It's probably been said already anyway. But regardless, I do think it begins to illustrate the train of thought I've been on recently. It all starts with a mild breakdown...

What happens when a sports car just won't cut it?

Mid-life crises come in many different shapes and sizes. But for a friend who ran a popular financial magazine, it came in the form of a question: am I selling my product in the right way? The answer he arrived at was no.

Effective though his methods were up to that point, he decided it just wasn't the right way. Confronted with the notion to "sell, or else," he chose "else". My friend set about reorganising things: searching for a new way to sell, an approach that would allow him to pass on a different message. He held meetings with various heads of department to discuss what the company was about. He invited people to paint their picture of the company. What were people proud of, he asked? Where did people see the company going, he wondered? Why did people even turn up for work at all? Naturally, the answers don't come easily: I think he's still looking for them.

At the time, the whole idea of asking such questions seemed a little silly. Just get on with it, was the default response. Sell, or else. But in thinking about what it takes to write good copy, I find myself thinking about these questions again... thinking about the soul searching process my friend attempted to go through. Perhaps it wasn't so silly.

This isn't the only crisis in confidence that I've witnessed. When reading a message distributed among information publishers in the US, I noticed that the writer was wondering if the sales material being produced wasn't a little too strongly geared towards Ogilvy's dictum: sell, or else. And by extension, screw the consequences. Again the company in question has a very effective network of sales experts. I'm talking about a collective that has sold millions as a direct result of copywriting – and in many cases, copywriting borne of the Ogilvy dictum. But they want to change it up. They're not quite sure how to do so at the moment. Still, the desire to change is certainly there.

What's going on? Is it just old men worrying about their legacy? Or is there something deeper? I'm swaying toward the later. And to explain why, let's turn away from the sellers and look at the buyers. You see, fact is: in the *age of the internet* the market has changed.

Not only do they know your game, they invented it

With each passing year, the market becomes increasingly aware of the cunning copy techniques we've so cleverly cultivated.

Alas. The fact is, markets change. Their awareness evolves. You only have to read your Eugene Schwartz to realize that – *yet again* – it's not a new problem. Indeed, I'm lucky to write a lot of copy for an international company that can afford to pay for reporting of such detail, it would make your eyes bleed. I get to see how the market is developing right now, through the slow sea change of open rates, click-through percentages and cart abandons. In fact, I've seen how click-through rates can fall where the copy is too aggressive and doesn't provide some form of value in itself. I've seen how conversion rates can double when you take the time to explain how something works before selling to people. I've seen copy fly in one country and fail in another all because the relationship hadn't been built with the customer. Consider it inside information: selling *above all else* is getting harder.

What's to be done? Should you still "sell, or else"? Or, as I suggest, should you in fact "share, or else"?

The day Gary Vaynerchuk took over the world

Gary Vaynerchuk isn't a god. And he can rub a lot of people up the wrong way. But make no mistake, he is very clever. He's clever because he makes predictions – and he believes in them come what may. He reminds me of an old newsletter writer, a chap called Gary

North (another Gary), who one of my mentors, Mark Ford, used to speak about.

It was rumoured Gary North was so convinced by claims of an imminent Y2K meltdown that he buried a tractor in preparation for the coming apocalypse. What he planned to do with the soiled JCB, I don't know. But I do know that despite his almighty misjudgement, his followers forgave him. Not just that – they continued to buy. Why? Because he evidenced the reasons for his belief so well and stuck so firmly by what he predicted. For Gary North, it wasn't just a case of "sell, or else" – he was sharing his story whether you wanted to believe it or not. I'm sure at the time selling wasn't his first priority.

Vaynerchuk is the same. For years now he's been predicting the rise of social media and its importance for businesses. He's made his case over and over – online, in books, from the stage, on TV – to the point where he's almost become a self-fulfilling prophecy. I feel like he's the personification of the dictum, "share, or else". If he hasn't coined it – he should. I've followed him for a while and aside from admiring his direct, my-way-or-the-high-way approach to marketing, what I think he's done most successfully is link his core marketing beliefs to the buzz phrase "social media". Whether he meant to do this or not is irrelevant. It's worked a dream either way. You see, when you scratch below the fact that social media is just another media (the clue is in the bloody name), you see what social media *really* represents is the market. And despite what various polls and infographics will have you believe, it's the same damn market there's always been: people who want to buy things from you.

One of a number of modern day ad men, Dave Trott, has wisely clocked on to this fact too. Trott's another very clever chap like Vaynerchuk. I saw him speak at a conference at the back-end of 2013. He pointed out that the media is irrelevant: the customer is a customer, whether you Facebook her, email her or cold call the poor woman all through the night. He drew a little picture. It made perfect sense.

Once we understand the market on social media is roughly the same market that was on your email list and that market was the same as the market on your direct mail lists, we understand that our market is now plugged-in whether we like it or not and they're ultra-aware of the world around them. That's the true lesson of social media. *Not* that you can get lots of people to buy Oreos if you tweet quickly during a super bowl commercial, but that the internet has truly broken out of the computer. Social media itself will die away in its prominence and merge with other media, but one fact will remain: the world now interacts in a way we've never known before.

We don't know how far it'll go. In *The Circle,* Dave Eggers describes a frighteningly possible, Google-style utopia – let's hope Eggers' imagination is just that. Either way, one thing we do know is that in this ultra-aware marketplace, "sell, or else" just isn't going to cut it.

I think the change in approach is inevitable. In truth, it's already happening. I believe we write to share. I believe that if our copy aims to educate as well as entice, in the long run we will sell more anyway. Right now, I'm advising copywriters to think about what they're *teaching* their readers as well as what they're trying to sell. I want readers to finish reading my copy feeling wiser. I want readers to take something away regardless of whether they make a purchase. More than that, as a copywriter, you are in a unique position to see a product or service from a different angle... you can see the end game, the ultimate benefits a person will derive from a product or service. And if those benefits aren't there, or you think there's something missing in the way the product is presented, you shouldn't sit quietly. You should look to help improve the product. Why? Because the better a product or service is, the easier it is to write copy for it.

You might think that's not your responsibility, it's beyond your remit, or that it's too much like hard work getting involved in product development and not worth your time. But this is bad thinking. By helping to improve a product you'll be able to write about it in a much more authentic way, which will ultimately result in a much stronger piece of copy. And on top of that, being seen as a copywriter who can help beyond their traditional role of the one who does the words will stand you ahead of other writers who only have a single string to their bow.

Don't get me wrong – you still need to sell. In that sense, Ogilvy is still on the money. But you shouldn't be so scared of his threat anymore – that "or else". I know that if I don't sell today, by *sharing* something useful or helping to improve the product or service, I'll more likely sell tomorrow, or the next day. Surely if I share my knowledge with you, you'll be more comfortable sharing your money with me, right? See, sharing's not so bad after all.

When you come to write your next piece of copy, let me offer you a new challenge: go out into the industry today and with a brave face…

Share, or else.

Top Tip

On the subject of sharing, it's important to remember copywriting can sometimes be like a lonely game. I admit the clichéd image of the lonesome writer in their ivory tower, crafting their latest masterpiece, is one I've no doubt subconsciously aspired to throughout my life. But, of course, it's nonsense. Turn to the acknowledgement page in any book and you'll see many people go into the process of writing a book than just the author themselves (this one is no exception).

It's the same for good copy. Good copy is not produced by a single person. It should be a collaborative effort, one that brings together lots of different minds and levels of experience to produce something that is, at the risk of sounding like a preacher, bigger than just one person. Next time you're tempted to lock yourself away with your laptop and an espresso machine, I suggest you avoid the restrictive and limited nature of working alone and look to collaborate with as many different minds as you can. Share your ideas. Do so and I guarantee your copy will be stronger.

Part Three

The
Interviews

Chapter Eighteen
The King of Research

> *"The writers who really succeed are almost always the ones who put the most time into researching."*
>
> — **John Forde**

The most well researched copywriter I know

John Forde's a bit cool. He'll hate me for saying, but it's true. He lives in Paris. He plays guitar. He has great taste in music. He can come up with big ideas off the cuff. And he is one of the best storytellers I know. But the one thing that really sets him apart from many of the best direct-response copywriters working today is his extraordinary discipline when it comes to research.

Being cool, he's also incredibly modest, but I don't think I've ever met another copywriter who does as much research into an idea as John does. Whenever I catch up with him he's always testing out some new Post-it note system or a fancy app that helps you keep track of notes, anything that might help him better record the little nuggets of inspiration he uncovers. His tireless commitment to research is one of the key reasons, I believe, he has been able to write so much great copy over the years, and continues to do so. It would be mind-blowing even to imagine just how many millions his writing has made. So let's not.

And of course, as John's cool, money's not really the thing he's interested in anyway. Like all truly great copywriters, he's interested in the ideas themselves. He revels in the research. He's excited by rambling discussions you have when digging into an idea. And he takes genuine pleasure in helping others to discover their own breakthrough ideas.

There's a lot you can learn from John and happily he shares some of it right in our conversation here.

A whole lot of luck

Glenn: John, let's start with a bit of background. For those at the back, what exactly do you do?

John: Officially, what I do now is write ad copy for financial products, at least most of the time. And all of those, in the info publishing area. Some of the time I also work with other writers to help copy chief their projects. And I help train the newbies. Outside of that, I also do some general consulting, assists during brainstorming, and a few speaking engagements throughout the year. Unofficially, I guess what you could say is that – some 26 or so years into this – I spend a lot of time reading, piling up more research than I need, and otherwise procrastinating my way through to finished projects, which I'll then go from thinking are perfect to feeling like I need to start all over again. I don't think that goes away.

Glenn: I know the feeling. No matter how long you've been writing copy, there's always that doubt with every new project.

John: Exactly. And really, what got me to this stage was really just a lot of luck, I'm sure. Just being in the right place at the right time and getting a chance to mentor with some great copywriters, Bill Bonner and Mark Ford. Though, to get in that lucky spot did require an all-day internship that paid $15 a day while I was also going to graduate school. Plus, listening to audiobooks – and we're talking cassettes at the time – from the other great marketers, while driving the hour to and from classes at night. I also put in my share of 10pm nights at the office, early in my career. Most nights I was still there when the janitor stopped by to say goodnight.

Glenn: But you're out of the office now?

John: Yeah. Most of the time I'm working out of home, either in the States or in our apartment in Paris. Or while travelling, either for work or because my wife is hooked on seeing new places. We've got a whole routine worked out for that, where I get up at 5am or so and work until noon, then we go get lunch with the kids and see the sights. It's a pretty good setup overall.

It's still a results business

Glenn: You're a direct-response copywriter and you pretty much always have been. It's a pretty weird niche… how'd you get into it?

John: Well, I think I was always drifting toward some kind of copywriting role. I've been a writer and avid reader for about as long as I can remember. And back in school, I had some vague idea that advertising might be a way to make money while still getting a chance to do something creative. But I didn't really have a clue early on that there was a difference in types of advertising that was only vaguely determined by the medium applied. When I first took a job that turned into a copywriter training position, it was for a publisher that did nothing but direct marketing. However, I didn't quite know what that was and it quickly became too late to ask without embarrassment. Of course, I gradually started to figure it out. Especially after the publisher I worked for buckled down and really started to track their mailing results. That's when you first get how direct-response works and, more importantly, what it's worth. Because with direct-response, of course, the ads don't just float out into the ether and hope to stir some later action. They command response then and there, on an individual basis. You're seeing results roll in, to the penny. It's a scary prospect at first because what if your copy flops, which it's absolutely going to some of the time. On the other hand, when copy works and you can measure exactly how well, that's really something.

Glenn: It's good you talk about the ability to measure results. It's something I've discussed at length in the book. What I think is really interesting though is how results-driven we are now in the so-called digital age and our background in direct-response has served us well.

John: Sure. Direct-response is extremely important. In fact, maybe more important than ever. After all, the people pushing the buttons or swiping up on tablet screens are more or less the same people who used to tear open envelopes. And even if they aren't, even if there's been a shift in generations, what motivates people is still pretty much the same – they want to be loved and respected, admired, safe and healthy, knowledgeable, validated, accomplished and successful. When they're angry, they want to feel heard. And they want evidence that supports their arguments, but well presented. It's nearly the same process when they're driven by fear. Yes, we're a bit less focused than before everything went online. Maybe we're a little more opinionated while being, surprisingly, a little less informed too. But all that does is turn up the heat and emotions that you need to tap and increase the speed at which you have to make your pitch. Because you're competing with so many more passionate, accessible messages than you used to in the age of print.

The age-old argument

Glenn: Now, I know it's silly to even attempt to discuss this here as we could talk for hours on this topic alone, but I would like to briefly get your thoughts on the long copy versus short copy debate... what's your view?

John: Yeah, it's the debate that will never die. Even though, in my opinion, you can pretty much put it to bed with a single word – trust. That's the reason direct-response copy runs long when it does. And it's also the reason that sometimes it runs shorter, though almost never as short as most of the ads you see on TV or spot on a nigh-on-wordless page of a glossy magazine. Meaning, those ads that do all their work with a slogan have their place and serve their function. But one thing they rarely do is close the sale. Instead of seeking any action on the spot, they set out to create a general abstraction of desire.

Glenn: I like that idea of trust. Have you spent long enough writing to the reader to earn their trust? It's a good way to think about how long your copy should be.

John: Of course, in direct-response if you don't ask for the sale at some point – more likely, at many points – during the pitch, you've failed. That's really something to ask of someone that you've stopped on the way from their front door to the trash can, in the case of print direct-response, or on their journey through a packed inbox or screen full of Facebook posts. No matter what ad you're putting in front of them, the undercurrent of what you're saying is always, "Wait, stop, look at me. I'm about to say something to you that you'll find so intriguing, so new, and so personally valuable that you'll not only give me enough of your time to explain to you what it is and why you should care, but that you'll want to pull out your credit card when I'm done to get yourself one of whatever I've got on offer." Again, that's a lot to ask. So much that it requires you to do more than just state the facts and list the price or ordering information. You need to build a relationship, one where the prospect trusts you've got something relevant and new to say... trusts you know what you're talking about... and trusts you can deliver on your promises. Doing that does take some well-chosen words, plunked down on the page in the right order, and more often than not it takes a lot of them. Because one quippy slogan does not a relationship make.

Glenn: Three cheers to that.

John: So, yes, it's not completely wrong to categorize 'direct-response copy' as equivalent to 'long copy', most of the time. That said, it's wrong to be so categorical. Because, of course, it's not just word count that makes any piece of copy work. If it were, that would be the basis of writer paycheck and freelancer royalty. Just like a car with a small engine can still outpace a bigger one if it's built right, direct-response copy that's more concise sometimes can to better than long copy. If and only if that shorter copy does a better job at hitting a relevant and emotionally rich target area for the prospect, if there's a great product and offer involved, and if it hits the sweet spot at exactly the right time in the prospect's life or when the market for an idea is particularly hot. Bottom line is that what works, works because of those reasons. The copy that works more often happens to run long is more of a symptom of that process than anything else.

Glenn: On the back of the idea of the misnomer of direct-response copy only being associated with long copy, I'd like to dispel another myth too. People tend to think direct-response is only useful for certain niches. Do you agree – or can any business use it to grow?

John: I guess there are situations where you might ask yourself if you need to go that extra mile and do all that work, for a product that might be so clear cut that even a regular ad in a shop window could make the sale. Say, for instance, if you were offering gallons of fresh milk at a good price. To write a sales letter, build a list and so on wouldn't seem necessary. Then again, never say never. David Ogilvy sold huge plots of real estate using direct-response tactics. You could even make a case that selling milk by direct-response might be justified, if – say – you were selling some kind of specialty milk for the lactose-intolerant, cruelty-free bovine enthusiast or something extra-fresh from a dairy with some staggeringly different and fascinating history. That's probably the key. Direct-response works great for carving out new territory in crowded space, by giving you room to change the perspective and tell the new story that nobody's telling. If that's something your product can do honestly and successfully, then yes direct-response could grow your business. Probably better than a more conventional, shorter, more abstract pitch.

Go to the customer

Glenn: Which do you think are the main factors for influencing behaviour and encouraging someone to respond directly to a piece of copy – long or short?

John: I think it's a pretty basic march right up the hierarchy-of-needs pyramid. At the most basic level, you're offering ways to help someone feel safe and cared for. They want their pain to be acknowledged, their fears and worries to be heard, and their suspicions and opinions to be validated. Especially the more emotionally dense ones. A little higher up the scale, they also want to be entertained. They want their sense of hope alighted. And they want to strive for something higher or greater. Which, by the way, is rarely just money or some physical transformation in themselves. Most of all, they want to be respected. Which, touchy-feely as it sounds, is just a form of love. We need people to care that we're alive and worth something. Clearly, every bit of what I just said there is less about what you're selling and more about who that person is and where they are whenever your pitch lands in front of them. And that, I think, is the real 'main factor' you're asking about. First and foremost, you can't influence anybody to do anything without focusing on who they are and who they'd like to become. You have to go meet them where they stand, rather than the other way around. Or you're dead at the starting gate. Once you've successfully figured that out, you start crafting your message so it fits that prospect profile. Take the most relevant claim, the one that will change that prospect's life in exactly the way he secretly hopes, and build it into a story he hasn't heard before. Something new so he'll actually enjoy listening and getting sold on something, even as he learns something new. We could reel off thousands of other tips, probably, but that's the big one.

Always be on the lookout

Glenn: Finally, John, you know I always say I admire you for the amount of research you do. But I wondered if it always starts there? Where do you begin the process of identifying an idea? And does it vary when you're writing a long copy sales letter to a short email advert?

John: I start anywhere I can, because those really great ideas are the goldmine. And they're going to jump out at you from everywhere. That means I've got to be reading and talking to people all the time, both in and out of the fields I write about most often. When I'm working on a project, a lot of ideas come out of brainstorming sessions and other conversations I have – and sometimes force – with the main characters connected with the product. A lot of times you'll discover they're sitting on ideas or things that could lead to a great idea, but don't know it. Though I guess the real place that I really start shaping the idea is on the page, while typing up research or – more often – when going back to edit what I wrote a day or two earlier. Even those are edits happening in my head, during a walk or a drive or a shower, it's the rare good idea that won't get even better, sharper, and more targeted during edits and critiquing sessions. That's why it's great for any writer, even experienced ones, to have a copy chief or someone similar to go to. Because getting the stuff on the page, while essential, is just like pouring the clay on the wheel. To really make something powerful out of it takes a more focused and sometimes group effort. When you get one of those lightning bolt, "This is a big idea!" moments that's great. But they don't happen often, even for the really great ad writers.

Glenn: You've just got to keep plugging away.

John: Exactly. The writers who really succeed are almost always the ones who put the most time into researching, rethinking, and reworking what they've come up with so far. Sometimes over and over again.

Chapter Nineteen
The Million Dollar Man

"All great ideas are simple."

— *Mark Ford*

You don't often meet millionaires

Growing up in a virtually abandoned fishing port on the east coast of England, I didn't get the chance to meet many millionaires. I say many. I didn't meet one. So when I first met Mark Ford, a genuine self-made multi-millionaire, I didn't quite know what to expect. A friend suggested I'd get on with him. I don't fully recall why, but I have a feeling it's because I was very sure of myself and, apparently, so was Mark. Of course, he had reason to be, I less so. Usually based in a quiet oceanfront village on the east coast of Florida, he was over in cold, dismal London to help improve the writing team I had just joined. I remember he spoke a lot, but not about what we were supposed to be talking about. I remember he challenged almost every 'norm' anybody attempted to hide behind. And I remember during the session breaks he would stand outside the building smoking a seriously expensive cigar. Yes, a proper, thick Havana cigar. But I remember most the conversation he had with me after the session. He told me I could write, that I had a good voice and if I stuck at it, I could do very good things. Being British and obscenely cynical about everything, I assumed this was a cunning motivational ruse and 'he said that to all the girls'. Still, it felt good to have this incredibly successful writer tell me I had what it takes. Motivational ruse or not, it worked and has spurred me on to where I am now. And over the decade that followed our first meeting, Mark has continued to offer me his extensive insight and generous support. So it's a pleasure to be able to share some of that insight directly with you here.

Times they are a changing

Glenn: Mark, you've been in the game for a long time now and you've been writing copy for many years. It seems a good place to start by asking how you've seen things change over the years? Or have they not changed?

Mark: There have been changes. Big changes. But there is also that which hasn't changed, which I'll get to in a moment.

The biggest change by far has been the internet. That drastically changed the direct marketing businesses I work with. In the old days of direct mail (prior to 2000), 90+% of our transactions – both marketing and fulfilment – occurred via mail delivery. That was slow and costly. Back then The Agora, for example, had about a million paid customers. To reach them, whether it was to send them a product or a sales letter or an invoice, it cost us about 50 cents in printing, paper and postage. So every contact with our full file cost us a half a million dollars. That was a huge expense – too much for us to absorb. So what we did was include advertising in every piece of mail we sent to our customers. We did that to "cover" the cost of the mailing. Because of this we couldn't contact our customers nearly as often as we do today, Back then we would contact our customers perhaps 20 times a year. Today we contact them 400 times or more. Which means we can give them many times more value for every dollar they spend. Which means that they become more responsive customers. Our customer lifetime values have more than doubled as a direct result of this frequency, which is a direct result of the de minimus cost of the internet.

The other important effect of the internet was speed. In the old, mail-order days it took weeks to get proper feedback from one's customers, either feedback from a survey or responses from a marketing effort. Today you can get feedback in minutes. This accelerated feedback loop has allowed our marketers to become much smarter, much more sophisticated and much more agile. It has made it much easier to deliver both products and promotions that appeal to the marketplace.

There are a hundred other smaller changes that are the result of these two. But there has also been something that has not changed. And that is human nature.

As we were first moving from print to digital publishing, there was a great deal of talk about how the internet was going to change the way people bought things – that the world of buying and selling, and particularly the consumer market, was going to change in a fundamental way. No longer would 'push' marketing (direct marketing) drive sales. Instead customers would decide what they want and need and find it by searching the web for appropriate websites ('pull' marketing). That did happen in certain sectors but some of us were quite sure it would never happen in our industry, which is about selling ideas. We believed for some obvious and some less obvious reasons that when it came to paying for information and advice, people would still need to be pushed a little. And that's exactly what happened. The web-based portion of our marketplace was and still is a very small piece of the pie. More than 80% of sales come from direct, outbound sales.

What those who predicted a change in our market failed to realize is that the first and most important event in the history of our relationship with our customers was the first 'pushed-out' marketing effort that provoked a sale.

Glenn: That's interesting, the idea that the sales copy is the primary relationship builder. People always think it's the product, the editorial copy in this case. But when you think about it, customers initially develop a relationship with the sales copy.

Mark: Exactly. Sales copy matters. That first marketing piece contained the ideas and the emotions and the language that motivated the customer to take action. Today, with the fast feedback loop I mentioned, it's much easier for information publishers to recognize this fact as true. But back then in the direct mail days there was often a big disconnect between marketing, copywriting and editorial. The editorial issues of the actual newsletter people subscribed to were often completely unrelated to the sales copy they'd read. And most people thought that was okay. The marketing pieces were supposed to be emotionally compelling. But the editorial products were supposed to be reasonable and rational and devoid of the big ideas and drama that made the promotional package work. It seldom occurred to publishers then that this was a serious mistake. Ironically, one of the most common complaints a publisher would hear was: "The first 'issue' was great. The issues since then are not." When we talked to them we found out that by the first issue they meant the promotional package. That's what they responded to. And that's what they expected (and wanted) to keep on getting. Today – because of the de minimus cost and nearly instant feedback loop of internet communications, it is much easier to understand what the customer wants and expects. And it is also much easier and cheaper to give that to him. We can give him more content. We can give him better content. And we can do so without feeling like we have to use the "hard pitch" any more. In other words, we can more easily provide value and work more on the principle of reciprocity.

The age of authenticity

Glenn: Now we can now communicate with customers on such a regular basis and you can start a conversation much earlier in the relationship, I'm interested in to hear if you think sales copy and editorial copy should be closer together?

Mark: I've always felt sales and editorial should collaborate much more closely. In fact, the closer they were in terms of content style and form the stronger the customer relationship would be. And now, because of the internet, its very easy for customers to compare the two, to see if you are giving him what he asked for and to determine whether you are the company and the person you said you were when you met (that first sales transactions).

If you do business online you must accept the fact that there will be loads of people out there that can see virtually everything you do, to figure out who you really are and what you are truly about. That's why transparency and authenticity are so important now. If you can be authentic both in your sales copy and your editorial copy by making them a unit, I think the chances of building a strong relationship is much better. There's the ATM promotion...that's a great example of this in practice.

Glenn: Sure, this is the idea that you go to your ATM and it won't let you draw any cash and you go to the shop and they won't accept cash and it paints a world where cash is essentially made redundant. It's based on the writer's view that the government and central banks want to take control of your money by abolishing cash.

Mark: That's the one. And it's a great example because there is nothing in the sales copy that misrepresents or diminishes the perspective of the writer, whose newsletter the story is meant to sell. The sales copy provides an engaging introduction to the big idea – and then the issues of the newsletter that they receive if they subscribe provide a continuity of the same ideas, the same passion and the same cleverness of expression. They end up getting exactly what they paid for.

Glenn: We're talking about a promotion for a newsletter written by Bill Bonner, the founder of The Agora. Wasn't the copy written by one of Bill's sons?

Mark: Yes it was. It was written by Jules, Bill's second son. When I first read it, it was so good and so much in Bill's natural voice that I was convinced that Bill himself wrote it. It was his son, but the ideas and the voice and everything else was the same.

Glenn: I'm really interested in the idea of authenticity in copy. On the face of it, writing to sell something you haven't created – *and in many cases doing so in someone else's voice* – seems utterly inauthentic. The very act of it! But as we know...the key to writing good copy lays in creating authenticity. It seems paradoxical almost?

Mark: It's not a very helpful one, but I think the answer is you simply have to be authentic in your writing. It shows through if you're not. If you are able to write authentically, that is so valuable as a tool. I'm not saying the authentic voice is the one that represents the true you, as others would see you. I think it means it's authentic to your own version of yourself. I'm saying this partly because of my own experience as a published author. I write on many subjects but my best known books and essays are about business and wealth building. In those books and essays I'm constantly giving advice. Some of the advice is based on the success I've had putting it to use. But some advice is nothing more than wishful thinking – what I think I should do. You'd think that giving advice about something you aren't yourself doing would come across badly, In fact, readers seem to respond very positively to my writing. And I think it's because they can tell – perhaps from my stories or my tone of voice or whatever – that I'm authentically interested in helping them and I'm giving them advice while being transparent about what I've done and failed (yet) to do.

And so if you have a voice and you can speak with sincerity and you can tell stories that convey emotion between what you're writing about and the reader's actual experience, I think the authenticity will come through. Though for all that, when it finally comes down to it, I think it helps if you just love your customer. When you're writing you need to have a genuine feeling that you are there to help your customer, to convey value to them, to share with them something they would have otherwise missed.

The FK score

Glenn: One of the more technical tools I remember you introduced me to when we first met was something called the FK score and it really helped me improve my own writing. It's a really useful tool used in the right way.

Mark: It is and I'm glad it was useful for you. The FK stands for Flesch-Kincaid. It was developed by two guys – Rudolf Flesch and J. Peter Kincaid – and it's a measure of the complexity of writing. It measures the number of polysyllabic versus monosyllabic words, the passive versus active construction of sentences, complex versus simple sentences. All the things we learned reading Strunk and White are kind of represented in this mathematical way of determining how difficult or complex the writing is. So, maybe you've heard this story before, but for people reading it's a good background. About 15–20 years ago, a very smart guy called Steve Sjuggerud came to work for The Agora and I gave him my little speech on the FK score and told him how important it was. Ten years or so later I invited Steve and a fellow editor, Alex Green, to give a talk about how to be a great editor. Both these guys were at the top of their game in terms of financial writers. Steve spoke about the FK speech I had given him and how, as someone who'd just received a PhD, he wasn't really interested in me telling him to dumb down his writing to meet a certain score. See, we aim for for a score – or 'grade' as it's known – lower than 7.5, but people tend to think it has something to do with a level of education. It doesn't. It has nothing to do with that. But anyway, Steve goes on to explain he went away and has been looking at this score ever since. More than that, he'd run a test on all the writers in the group, including Bill Bonner and myself. He found there was almost a 100% correlation between high loyalty from readers and responses from readers and low FK scores. In fact, he said the two people who had the lowest FK scores of the group he studied were Bill and I. I was proud of that. Of course, Bill was very upset. He didn't like the idea his writing has a low FK score. I mean, it just shows you how people don't get it. But the FK score forces you to write simply and to express your idea simply. Indeed, if your idea is good, you should be able to express it simply and if you do, it will become a beautiful idea. All great ideas tend to be simple.

Glenn: That is very true.

Mark: Yet so many people dislike this idea of writing and articulating their idea in a simple way. I've heard every reason why somebody can't get their FK score below 7.5. But when you say that, it's only because you are not writing well enough. I can tell you when I'm writing an essay and I think *Oh man, I am so smart, this is so clever…*then I run the FK score and it's 11. I used to think, screw it, I'm going to publish it anyway. But later I'd look again and realise I didn't know what I was trying to say and it was a bad piece. So now, if I can't get the score down to 7.5 or below, I know it's because I haven't done the thinking and I need to think some more.

Articulate one idea at a time

Glenn: What advice do you have for helping writers better articulate their ideas?

Mark: One thing I can say is that when I write, I try to follow the rule of one. You already use this, right?

Glenn: I do, and I've covered it in the book. It's one of the best pieces of advice you ever gave me.

Mark: I'm glad. And of course, it's very simple. You should only write about one thing at a time and by 'time' I mean if it's an essay, it should be an essay about one thing and not 12 things. If it's an advert, it should look from one angle. If it's a sales letter, it should be about one single idea. I just talked about Steve and Alex giving presentations. Alex had a brilliant presentation on 12 ideas that day too, yet not a single one of them I remember today. But I still remember Steve's. He only talked about one thing and everybody in attendance left the talk and put it into practice. That's the rule of one in action. To do this, you need to figure out how to articulate your idea in the simplest way, almost in a single sentence. A single, emotionally compelling sentence. On top of that you build the story, a story that illustrates the idea before you actually explain it. You'll notice, if you get it right, when you're able to articulate your idea in the simplest way and you're able to build a story around it, the story part will always end up around a 4 on the FK grade scale. It'll be the rest of the argument, the copy you've not thought through properly that is causing a higher FK score.

Glenn: And you're quite tough on the use of the score, right?

Mark: As a publisher, or as an editor, I wouldn't ever allow anybody to send me stuff to edit if the FK wasn't 7.5 or below. I'm not being a jackass when I insist on that. It's just that I know from experience it would just be a total waste of both of our time. The first thing I do when anyone submits something to me, is check the FK score. And that goes for anyone…even if it was the best copywriter working today…I'd send it back. I'm not going to read it because I know beforehand there will be so much work to do because the idea won't have been figured out yet. As a copywriter, it's your responsibility to figure out the idea and how to express it.

Glenn: I like that. It's hard and I know from experience when I've checked my own writing and it's just above 7.5, my instinct is to leave it. But that's lazy and it's probably going to mean the copy is weaker… and for an obvious reason.

Mark: We all do it. But if you can maintain the discipline to check yourself and overcome that instinct, you'll write stronger copy. It's as simple as that.

Chapter Twenty
A Friend from Down Under

"There is no real secret to it. You've just got to go and read everything you can."

— **James 'Woody' Woodburn**

You don't have to drink, but it helps

When I first moved to London to begin my career as a direct-response copywriter, one of the only friends I had in the office, a great writer called Tommy Orme, left pretty soon after I started. It meant I had to find another friend in the office. Unfortunately, that ended up being James Woodburn, or Woody, as pretty much everyone knows him. He hadn't been writing copy for much longer than me at the time, but he 'got it' as we used to say and learning the ropes with him was a big help in my own education. I say our meeting was 'unfortunate' because my liver didn't do so well out of our meeting. We drank so often in one London pub, one night the landlord paid our bill as a reward for our loyalty. We both realised, though the gesture was a kind one, it was a sign we were probably in there a bit too often. Livers willing, we worked together for about four years in London before Woody decided to 'up sticks' and move to Australia. Whether that was to get away from me, we'll never truly know. Either way, it was a good move. He's written some truly breakthrough direct-response copy and most recently helped launch the US Agora Financial business in Australia, which is doing great things under his leadership. As well as continuing to be a good friend, Woody is one of the copywriters I always look to for opinion and insight on my own copy and I often collaborate closely with him on projects. In our conversation here,

Woody shares some excellent insight into the process of writing direct-response copy.

It was all an accident

Glenn: Let's start with the basics: who are you and how long you have been writing copy?

Woody: Well, my name is James Woodburn, though everyone calls me Woody. These days I run Agora Financial in Australia. But I started writing copy in...I think it was in 2006... something like that. You want to know how I came to write copy?

Glenn: Already we can see your amazing storytelling prowess coming into action. Yes, that's what I just asked you.

Woody: Ha. Well I came into writing copy by accident. Probably like most people do. I don't know anyone who goes to University and wants to be a copywriter. It's not really a job that's talked about. So, I just started writing when I was applying for University. I wasn't really sure what to do. I knew I wanted to do either art or something to do with writing. I decided to go the writing route. I still didn't know what to do at the end of the course, so I thought I'd train to be a journalist and just basically drinking solidly for six months while trying to be a journalist. I quickly realized after about two weeks it wasn't for me. By chance I came across an advert for The Agora, which was unlike any other advert I'd really seen before. There was something different about it. I applied, got an interview and got the job. It was actually a role in the editorial department, for a newsletter at the time called *FTSE Trader*.

Glenn: That's interesting... you actually started out writing editorial?

Woody: Yeah, and I must admit I didn't know I was doing. I just knew I needed to get out of being a journalist. I couldn't believe I actually got the job, but there I was. I really enjoyed coming into work and I liked the challenge. But something wasn't clicking. So I started trying to write the adverts in the emails that got sent out. Suddenly I realised, *oh I quite like this* and it was kind of cool. I asked the publisher how my adverts were doing and they were doing well, getting quite a few clicks. Eventually, I found myself spending more time writing adverts than editorial and the publisher suggested I move over into the copywriting team.

Obsession can be a good thing

Glenn: So you started to work on bigger projects?

Woody: It took a little while as I was working as part of a really established team. People like Mike Graham, Dan Denning and Simon Munton, who I still work with now in Australia. I knew I was going to basically write whatever I was given. So my first real project was down to a mistake. Some junior marketers had bought about 5,000 soap pods or something he had about 4,000 left in the warehouse. My task was to try and shift them. The copy I wrote smashed it and we shifted them. But more importantly, that's when I realised I loved copy. I realised it was something I could get my teeth into and really get super obsessive about one thing and try to convince myself why I need it.

Glenn: Obsession is a good word to use there, because it's something I've always said is one of your biggest strengths as a copywriter: you get super obsessive over the things you write about. One key skill when it comes to writing good copy is identifying what it is about what you're selling that even experts on that thing are intrigued. To identify that unique element, you've got to go pretty deep. What's your process there... how do you become obsessed, so to speak?

Woody: Reading, lots of reading. There is no real secret to it. You've just got to go and read everything you can about the topic directly but also indirectly. So, just take the copy for the soap pod I just mentioned. I was given a ton of proof... articles in *The Sun*, the *Daily Mail*, and there are all the readers who've used it. But it all felt like surface proof. It wasn't very emotional. I wanted to find the story behind the story. So I started reading about where the soap came from and found it came from somewhere in Transylvania or something and there were special qualities about this particular type that they put in that you won't find in any other country or any other region. I probably over researched but it's worth it.

Glenn: I want to point out here that you are not writing a single piece of copy at this first stage, you are just looking, you're learning, you're figuring things out.

Woody: I always start out by trying to write something but you quickly get frustrated because you don't really understand what you're trying to write. That is a very quick route to writing weak copy. You need to kind of fill your mind. You need to fill your mind with everything related to the topic and only then will something come out that's worth writing.

Glenn: And assuming you've got that thing worth writing, what's your next move from there?

Woody: Sometimes you get a key idea or a key phrase that you keep coming back to but you can't formulate it. I think at this stage it's best to just write as much down as possible. Sometimes I'll write a headline that is really long and then you go ahead and write more out and you come back for the headline and chisel it. You've got to always be editing and revising. Chiselling your copy down will make it stronger. What I also like to do is after I have really delved in and written some copy I'm happy with, I like to have a meeting with someone who understands the principle or what we are trying to do but they're not connected to the copy in the slightest. I had a big hit with a long copy letter called 'The Sixth Revolution'. That came out of just me and another writer called Dan Denning talking about the idea. A lot of time, the words I use in the copy don't come from me, it comes from the person I'm talking to. They soak in what I'm saying and they might chime in with something and I will be like *Ah, that's the phrase*. After that, I just write out the copy as best I can.

Reading aloud

Glenn: Once you've finished the copywriting itself and you've got a draft, what's your process then?

Woody: I always get the editor, or whoever you're writing the copy for, involved to read it. Sure, there are some editors I've worked with who are really good editors and understand what you're trying to do with the copy, but they are not copywriters. They will start trying to over prove something or think that a reader new to the idea you're writing about is going to think about it in the same way they are, which is probably not the case. But still, you need to go through this process with every piece of copy you write. If not the editor, someone else needs to read it. Aside from the few 'editorial' issues you might have, the process is really useful for adding authenticity to your copy. We will go into a meeting room and I will literally get the editor to read the copy aloud. It very quickly becomes apparent when a sentence is bumbling or if a paragraph loses your interest. I've done this many times and often find there's edits on every single page. But it just makes the copy so much stronger.

Glenn: That's really interesting. I always encourage the writer to read the copy aloud but you specifically get the editor to do it too?

Woody: Definitely. And not just with long copy. Do it with everything. When you read copy aloud, you can hear whether something is finished, whether you've got your message across, whether you are going on too long.

Great ideas and where to find them

Glenn: OK. So let me ask you an impossible question: how do you find good ideas?

Woody: How do you find them?

Glenn: Yes, in less than 100 words. Maybe a better way to put it: how did you come up with the idea for the last piece of copy you just wrote?

Woody: That's more manageable. In fact, I can tell you straight… just reading and talking to people about it. You quickly know if you're hitting cold with a certain idea if the other person is bored when you're talking about it. Remember the event you held in London a while back… all about ideas?

Glenn: I do. I organised it.

Woody: It was actually good. I was expecting it to be terrible because you were organising it… but it was great. Anyway, I remember I came along with my editor here and we came loaded with ideas. We had about eight different ones that we were excited by. I think we put six in the presentation we gave but there was one idea that I noticed a palpable change in the audience. I just saw everyone's interest pick up in the room. And more specifically, I think it was Ryan McGrath (a US copywriter) who literally stood up to ask me a question about it before we'd even finished talking. The idea clearly stuck a nerve. So I guess that's a good starting point… if you can have a conversation with people completely unrelated to your market or what you're thinking about and they're really interested in the idea beyond any monetary promise, beyond any the stocks going up… if there is an idea that gets people interest… that is a probably a good starting point.

Glenn: Great. And to put a really practical angle on it, we're basically saying here to test your ideas in front of people because deep down, you will know when you get someone's attention.

A final thought

Glenn: To finish off, I want you to give us your biggest and best copywriting tip to anyone looking to improve their copywriting skills… what is your one Desert Island Discs-type takeaway?

Woody: Don't try to write copy like you think copy should sound. Does that make sense? It's a really big problem a lot of junior copywriters, marketers and editors have. They're good writers but then the moment they try to write a piece of copy their voice completely changes. It becomes cheesy. It becomes salesman-like. It becomes superficial, essentially just shouting. It's because they think copy has to be like that... but it doesn't. Understand what you are trying to say, find the most interesting and exciting, useful and valuable and unique way of explaining it... and then just say it as you would if you were explaining it to your dad. Just be authentic.

Glenn: Lovely stuff. And the perfect thought to end on.

Chapter Twenty One
Psst... One More Thing

> *"There are a couple of loose ends I'd like to tie up. Nothing important you understand."*
>
> **— Peter Falk as Columbo**

The Columbo technique

The crook would think they'd got away with the perfect crime. They'd outwitted the bumbling Columbo. But then bang! He'd turn around on his way out the room and deliver his famous line: "Just one more thing." And it would be that inconspicuous thing that would unravel the crime, stitch up the crook and leave Columbo victorious. Hurrah!

Adding just one more thing, like Columbo, at the end of your copy in the form of a postscript or PS can significantly increase your response. A PS in a piece of copy gives you a final chance to argue the case for the product you're selling or point you're making. If the main body of your message has done its job, by this point the reader is almost ready to click. The PS should provide one more piece of information that makes your product or service irresistible. But here a lot of people often slip up and miss a great opportunity.

You see, your PS can reaffirm something that you've mentioned already. In this case it acts as a final reminder of the claims you've made, or the proof you've provided. But. I believe this doesn't maximise the potential of your PS.

Think about it. You've already made your point and the reader will have judged it valid or invalid. Just repeating it isn't going to make a whole lot of difference. We see examples of this *repetition is equivalent to truth* in daytime discussion shows. Next time you see some C-list celebrity trying to make a point, notice how they repeat everything twice under the illusion that doing so somehow makes it more real. To avoid making this mistake, instead of wasting the PS opportunity by repeating something in your main message, save one piece of information to exclusively reveal in the PS.

Make your final word irresistible

What exclusive information can you save for your PS – or put another way, what can you afford to leave out of your main message? Naturally, this all depends on your product or service. You should already have a good idea of the benefits of your product or service and I'd recommend making a list of them on a separate piece of paper. If you've got a list of six great benefits then you can likely afford to leave one for the PS and use the others in the body of the message. But if you think all the benefits of the product or service need to be communicated in the main message, there are another two options open to you.

Firstly, as a PS you could include testimonials from people who have already tried your product or service. This is a great way to further prove the case for what you're selling. If the reader is already sold on the idea, the fact that you've only included these testimonials almost as an afterthought will further prove how good your product or service is.

Your second option is to introduce in the PS a money-back guarantee. By this point, a reader will be one of: (a) very interested; (b) still not sure; or (c) completely uninterested. Reader A will see the money-back guarantee as a bonus. Reader B may see the money-back guarantee as a reason to at least give your product or service a go. As too might Reader C, but if they don't, nothing you could have done at this point would have made a difference.

You can see how useful a PS can be and testing has proven that including one does increase sales. But be warned. Overusing a PS will dilute its power. Like a band who always come on to do an encore, readers will expect it and might start to skip it – assuming you're going to say the same thing as last time. To really make the most of your final word, keep it spontaneous, keep it fresh and make sure it's irresistible.

Top Tip

What? No, that's it. We're done. It's over. We've reached the end. Surely I've covered enough for you? OK. One *final* tip. Here's how you can really supercharge your PS. You see, the PS is like a little secret down at the bottom. One not everyone sees. So, you can further support this sense of secrecy by introducing your PS with a "Psst". It's quirky, I know, but seeing that "Psst" there always gets my attention. It's a classic.

Acknowledgements

Thank you to all the copywriters and marketers who have helped me further my understanding of this weird art. Specifically, my thanks to Dave Fedash for giving me my first break in the industry and to the *Goodfellas*, Darren Hughes and Vinod Gorasia, who helped turn it into a career.

Thank you to Bill Bonner and Addison Wiggin for creating a company that helps people like me do things they never imagined they could.

A special thank you to John Forde, Mark Ford and James Woodburn for agreeing to be part of this book and taking the time to talk to me about their own experience. And also my thanks for their continued inspiration, instruction and support.

I am deeply indebted to my editor at Harriman House, Craig Pearce. Turns out writing a book is a lot different to writing copy, and his patience and guidance throughout the process was illuminating.

Finally, thank you to my partner, Ruth, and my family for the ongoing support, reassurance and reality checks. Oh, and a nod to my dog, Pablo, for his silent patience in allowing me to finish *just one more paragraph* before his morning walk.